GUARD
OUR UNBELIEF

GUARD
OUR UNBELIEF

Passages for Discussion

selected by

J. J. EVANS
Headmaster, Strode's School, Egham

OXFORD UNIVERSITY PRESS

Oxford University Press, Ely House, London W.1

GLASGOW NEW YORK TORONTO MELBOURNE WELLINGTON
CAPE TOWN DELHI IBADAN NAIROBI DAR ES SALAAM LUSAKA ADDIS ABABA
BOMBAY CALCUTTA MADRAS KARACHI LAHORE DACCA
KUALA LUMPUR SINGAPORE HONG KONG TOKYO

First published 1971
Reprinted 1974

And now what are we? Unbelievers both,
Calm and complete, determinately fixed
Today, tomorrow and for ever, pray?
You'll guarantee me that? Not so, I think!
In no wise! All we've gained is, that belief,
As unbelief before, shakes us by fits,
Confounds us like its predecessor. Where's
The gain? How can we guard our unbelief,
Make it bear fruit to us?—there's the problem here.

Robert Browning,
Bishop Blougram's Apology

Printed in Great Britain by Richard Clay (The Chaucer Press) Ltd,
Bungay, Suffolk

PREFACE

Almost insuperable difficulties face the effective teaching of Religious Knowledge today. In an age when there is so much uncertainty in orthodox Christianity about the metaphysics (if any) it adheres to, about the morals it ought to teach, and about the imagery and language it ought to use, and when so much scepticism faces the accredited spokesmen of any institution, it is not surprising that any religious instruction based on traditional lines should meet with suspicion and apathy. Furthermore, in the United Kingdom the status of Religious Knowledge as a valid 'subject' is compromised by the 'kiss of death' of statutory obligation; and often it is regarded by pupils, if only unconsciously, as somehow part of an adult conspiracy to encourage good behaviour which can safely be ignored after leaving school. A possible solution to this predicament became clear to me personally when I became aware that the most fruitful discussions on religion took place when I was teaching English or Classics and not 'R.K.' When faced, outside the context of 'R.K.', with some fundamental human problem raised by some great writer with no particular axe to grind, a class seldom fails to respond with deep interest and liveliness. This book is intended to provide reading matter for such discussions both in sixth forms and colleges of further education.

Of course, most teachers of Religious Knowledge have already had recourse to free discussion as a solution to their problems. Most of these discussions have a moral or humanist basis, 'How ought human beings to *behave* to one another?' This book is an attempt to take the discussions a stage further back, to the question, 'What can I *believe*?' It contains a number of passages written in the main by writers of international reputation who deal seriously and profoundly with the problems of good and evil, of belief and unbelief, and of the human personality in the modern world; they are passages written by those who are primarily novelists and dramatists, and not Christian apologists. This fact has, in my experience, taken them out of the context where they can safely be ignored.

This book does not aim to guide its readers along any particular line of belief, but rather to develop a quality of imagination profound enough to make an adequate response to the problems of belief whenever they arise. This quality of imagination is of particular importance in an age when the element of agnosticism inherent in faith is more freely acknowledged than formerly, and to a generation burdened (if that is not too strong a word) with the task of living up to its reputation of 'thinking things out for itself'. It is important to face the likelihood that most of those now being taught in schools and colleges will in a few years adopt a position which is more or less agnostic; it is vital that this agnosticism should not be a superficial one—and a superficial agnosticism is often the reaction of those who have been prepared only for orthodox religious beliefs. How often one hears, on television discussions for example, such expressions of easy agnosticism from those who have left religion at the first experience of a difficulty, from people whose imaginations can measure up to the magnitude of problems in economics, say, or sociology, but not to the magnitude of problems of religious belief. Such people often remain in a static condition of adolescent agnosticism at the level of 'I cannot believe in a God who allows wars'. One wishes that they had read the outburst of Ivan against evil in *The Brothers Karamazov*, or Camus's account of a dying child in *The Plague*. Shocks to belief would not then have been encountered unprepared. Like the spectators of Greek tragedy, they might have been 'purged of pity and terror' at one level and so enabled to take a step further into a deeper agnosticism or faith.

I hope that the choice of passages is sufficiently wide for the teacher to make his own selection. In the earlier stages of preparing this book, I was apprehensive that the prevailing mood of *angst* in the literature I examined might produce a book unutterably gloomy in its outlook; but I have included writers who could be classed as 'optimistic', and if it appears that I have included one or two passages as light relief, I hope that this is not unwelcome. If some of the writers do not measure up to the international stature I have claimed for them, either on the grounds of quality or repute, I can only say that my experience of the reactions to them by my pupils justifies their inclusion.

The extracts are necessarily of varying lengths, but in most cases it has been possible to divide them into sections short enough to be read during a session while still allowing some time for discussion afterwards. In the case of the longer extracts, it will be necessary for the class to read them on their own before the lesson. I hope

that the mere reading of the extracts themselves will arouse discussion. But I have suggested a few points for discussion; these
vary a good deal in difficulty and their use is left to the teacher's
discretion; I certainly do not intend that they should all be worked
through. Some may lend themselves to written answers. Each group
of extracts is prefaced by an introduction which explains the context and gives some biographical detail about the author; some of
these introductions contain ideas which may be useful in discussion
and it is therefore necessary that the students should read them
carefully before the extracts.

Finally, I must express my gratitude to my colleagues and
friends who have helped with advice and encouragement in the
preparation of this book, and in particular to Mr. Michael Mere-
dith and Mr. Howard Moseley, both of Eton College, who read
the manuscript with great care and who offered many valuable
suggestions, most of which I have gratefully adopted. My debt to
them is considerable.

CONTENTS

ACKNOWLEDGEMENTS

The author and publisher gratefully acknowledge permission to reproduce the following copyright material:

Samuel Beckett: *Waiting for Godot*. Reprinted by permission of Faber and Faber Ltd. and Grove Press Inc. Translated from the original French text by the Author. Copyright © 1954 by Grove Press Inc.

Albert Camus: *The Plague* translated by Stuart Gilbert. Copyright © Librairie Gallimard, translation copyright © 1948 by Stuart Gilbert (Hamish Hamilton, London).

Joyce Cary: *The Captive and The Free*. Reprinted by permission of Michael Joseph Ltd.

C. P. Cavafy: 'Waiting for the Barbarians' and 'Ithaka' from *Selected Poems* translated by P. Sherrard and E. Keeley. Reprinted by permission of Deborah Rogers Ltd., London, on behalf of the Estate of Constantine Cavafy and Mrs Singopoulo.

Marc Connelly: *Green Pastures*. Reprinted by permission of Delisle Ltd.

F. M. Dostoevsky: *The Brothers Karamazov* translated by David Magarshack. Reprinted by permission of Penguin Books Ltd.

Margaret Drabble: *The Millstone*. Reprinted by permission of Weidenfeld & Nicolson Ltd.

Petru Dumitriu: *Incognito*. Reprinted by permission of Collins, Publishers.

E. M. Forster: *A Passage to India* and *The Hill of Devi*. Reprinted by permission of Edward Arnold (Publishers) Ltd.

Graham Greene: *The Lawless Roads* and *The Power and the Glory*. (William Heinemann Ltd.). Reprinted by permission of Laurence Pollinger Ltd.

Aldous Huxley: *Brave New World*. Reprinted by permission of Mrs. Laura Huxley and Chatto and Windus Ltd.

H. Ibsen: *Brand* translated by M. Meyer. (Rupert Hart-Davis Ltd.) Reprinted by permission of David Higham Associates Ltd.

Eugene Ionesco: *Rhinoceros* translated by Derek Prouse. Reprinted by permission of Calder and Boyars Ltd.

Arthur Koestler: *Darkness at Noon* translated by D. Hardy. Reprinted by permission of Jonathan Cape Ltd.

Rose Macaulay: *The Towers of Trebizond*. Reprinted by permission of Collins, Publishers.

Paul Tillich: *The Shaking of the Foundations*. Reprinted by permission of S.C.M. Press Ltd. and Charles Scribner's Sons. Copyright 1948 Charles Scribner's Sons.

J. Neville Ward: *The Use of Praying*. Reprinted by permission of Epworth Press.

Evelyn Waugh: *The Loved One*. (Chapman and Hall.) Reprinted by permission of A. D. Peters & Co.

John Whiting: *The Devils*. (William Heinemann Ltd.) Reprinted by permission of A. D. Peters & Co.

Charles Williams: *Descent into Hell*. Reprinted by permission of David Higham Associates Ltd.

1. ALBERT CAMUS

THE PLAGUE

ALBERT CAMUS was born in Algeria in 1913. His father was killed very shortly afterwards in the battle of the Marne and he was brought up by his mother, who was Spanish. He read philosophy at the University of Algiers and took his *licence* there, but tuberculosis cut short any further academic work and he came to Europe in 1937 in order to rest. This was his first visit, but he returned later on and took up journalism. During the German occupation of France he was active in resistance work and became editor of the secret paper *Combat*. Among his earlier works were a play, *Caligula* (1939), a novel, *The Outsider* (1942), and a long essay, *The Myth of Sisyphus* (1942). In the immediate post-war years he produced more plays and a steady output of novels, essays, and political articles. *The Plague* appeared in 1947 and another novel, *The Fall,* in 1956. In 1957 Camus was awarded the Nobel Prize for Literature. He was killed in a car accident in France in 1960.

A fairly widespread current attitude towards religion is that of scepticism, whether superficial or profound, or even cynicism; there is a feeling that the beliefs so strongly held by previous generations are no longer intellectually acceptable, and that modern science has revealed them to be illusions. For some, this disillusionment has gone further and it has seemed that life itself is entirely meaningless and futile. Camus was, for an important part of his life, in the forefront of this nihilistic philosophy. In *The Myth of Sisyphus* he wrote:

> ... in a universe that is suddenly deprived of illusions ... man feels a stranger. He is an irremediable exile, because he is deprived of memories of a lost homeland as much as he lacks the hope of a promised land to come. This divorce between man and his life, the actor and his setting, constitutes the feeling of Absurdity.

By 'Absurdity' Camus does not mean 'ridiculousness'; originally the word 'absurd' meant 'harsh' or 'out of tune' and Camus uses it to mean all that is out of harmony with man's reason, his natural hopes and aspirations. He uses this term to cover all those experiences which run contrary to our sense of what is just and fair, and which upset our desire for happiness and our need to find meaning in our existence. He writes in *The Myth of Sisyphus* of such examples of the Absurd as the deadening routine of much modern industrial life, the 'otherness' of people and even of an element in ourselves, and the waste of so much human potential in apparently arbitrary sudden death and prolonged suffering.

Camus's novel *The Plague*, from which the following extract comes, is on the surface a straightforward account of an outbreak of bubonic plague in Oran in the 1940s as recorded by an intelligent observer, Jean Tarrou, who happened to be there at the time. But it is far more than that; it provides a theme on which Camus can work out his worries and anxieties about the human condition, and the plague itself is a symbol of the Absurd. Some critics have seen the plague as representing the evil of the German occupation of France; others have more broadly interpreted it as being 'whatever we think it is—whatever the reader happens to regard as the ultimate opposition to the human will, all modes and sources of death.'

But Camus's philosophy did not stop here; he refused to accept the Absurd. One of his key-phrases was 'Lutte toujours', and for the remainder of his life he did indeed strive towards a more hopeful humanism. In one of his essays, written in 1954, he wrote:

> We know that we are victims of a dilemma; that we must refuse to accept it and do what is necessary to eradicate it. Our task as men is to find some formulas to pacify the great anguish of mankind. We must put together what has been torn apart, make justice a possibility in an obviously unjust world, render happiness meaningful to peoples poisoned by the sufferings of our age.

Camus, as this extract will show, faced up to and accepted the worst aspects of life before attempting to outline some positive reaction to them. But he was too aware of the complexities of the human condition today to offer any hint of a 'solution'. It is tantalizing to imagine what position Camus might have reached had his life been longer. But his own comment on his position is perhaps worth more than any such speculation: 'The difference between me and the nihilists ... is that I believe in a truth and am searching for it; I believe that the search *is* the truth.'

This extract describes the agonising death from the plague of a small child, the son of M. Othon, the police magistrate; the main characters are Rieux, a doctor who plays a leading part in helping to control the plague and who reflects Camus's own philosophy, and Paneloux, a Jesuit priest, who in the early stages of the outbreak had preached a sermon in which he proclaimed his belief that the plague had come as an act both of judgement and of love from God. The small amount of time that the people of Oran had previously devoted to God, he said, had not been enough to sate 'the fierce hunger of his love. He wished to see you longer and more often; that is his manner of loving and indeed it is the only manner of loving. And that is why, wearied of waiting for you to come to Him, He loosed on you this visitation. . . .'

The death of Monsieur Othon's Son

Towards the close of October Castel's anti-plague serum was tried for the first time. Practically speaking, it was Rieux's last card. If it failed, the doctor was convinced the whole town would be at the mercy of the epidemic, which would either continue its ravages for an unpredictable period, or perhaps die out abruptly of its own accord.

The day before Castel called on Rieux, M. Othon's son had fallen ill and all the family had to go into quarantine. Thus the mother, who had only recently come out of it, found herself isolated once again. In deference to the official regulations, the magistrate had promptly sent for Dr. Rieux the moment he saw symptoms of the disease in his little boy. Mother and father were standing at the bedside when Rieux entered the room. The boy was in the phase of extreme prostration and submitted without a whimper to the doctor's examination. When Rieux raised his eyes he saw the magistrate's gaze intent on him, and, behind, the mother's pale face. She was holding a handkerchief to her mouth, and her big, dilated eyes followed each of the doctor's movements.

'He has it, I suppose?' the magistrate asked in a toneless voice.

'Yes.' Rieux gazed down at the child again.

The mother's eyes widened yet more but she still said nothing. M. Othon, too, kept silent for a while before saying in an even lower tone:

'Well, doctor, we must do as we are told to do.'

Rieux avoided looking at Mme. Othon, who was still holding her handkerchief to her mouth.

'It needn't take long,' he said rather awkwardly, 'if you'll let me use your phone.'

The magistrate said he would take him to the telephone. But, before going, the doctor turned towards Mme. Othon.

'I regret very much indeed, but I'm afraid you'll have to get your things ready. You know how it is.'

Mme. Othon seemed disconcerted. She was staring at the floor. Then, 'I understand,' she murmured, slowly nodding her head. 'I'll set about it at once.'

Before leaving, Rieux on a sudden impulse asked the Othons if there wasn't anything they'd like him to do for them. The mother gazed at him in silence. And now the magistrate averted his eyes.

'No,' he said; then swallowed hard. 'But . . . save my son.'

In the early days a mere formality, quarantine had now been reorganized by Rieux and Rambert on very strict lines. In particular they insisted on having members of the family of a patient kept apart. If, unawares, one of them had been infected, the risks of an extension of the infection must not be multiplied. Rieux explained this to the magistrate, who signified his approval of the procedure. Nevertheless, he and his wife exchanged a glance which made it clear to Rieux how keenly they both felt the separation thus imposed on them. Mme. Othon and her little girl could be given rooms in the quarantine hospital under Rambert's charge. For the magistrate, however, no accommodation was available except in an isolation camp the authorities were now installing in the Municipal Sports Ground, using tents supplied by the Highways Department. When Rieux apologized for the poor accommodation, M. Othon replied that there was one rule for all alike, and it was only proper to abide by it.

The boy was taken to the Auxiliary Hospital and put in a small ward, which had formerly been a junior classroom. After some twenty hours Rieux became convinced that the case was hopeless. The infection was steadily spreading, and the boy's body putting up no resistance. Tiny, half-formed, but acutely painful buboes were clogging the joints of the child's puny limbs. Obviously it was a losing fight.

Under the circumstances Rieux had no qualms about testing Castel's serum on the boy. That night, after dinner, they performed the inoculation, a lengthy process, without getting the slightest reaction. At daybreak on the following day they gathered round the bed to observe the effects of this test inoculation on which so much hung.

The child had come out of his extreme prostration and was tossing about convulsively on the bed. From four in the morning Dr. Castel and Tarrou had been keeping watch and noting, stage by stage, the progress and remissions of the malady. Tarrou's bulky form was slightly drooping at the head of the bed, while at its foot, with Rieux standing beside him, Castel was seated, reading, with every appearance of calm, an old leather-bound book. One by one, as the light increased in the former classroom, the others arrived. Paneloux, the first to come, leant against the wall on the opposite side of the bed to Tarrou. His face was drawn with grief, and the accumulated weariness of many weeks, during which he had never spared himself, had deeply seamed his somewhat prominent forehead. Grand came next. It was seven o'clock, and he apologized for being out of breath; he could only stay a moment, but wanted to know if any definite results had been observed. Without speaking, Rieux pointed to the child. His eyes shut, his teeth clenched, his features frozen in an agonized grimace, he was rolling his head from side to side on the bolster. When there was just light enough to make out the half-obliterated figures of an equation chalked on a blackboard that still hung on the wall at the far end of the room, Rambert entered. Posting himself at the foot of the next bed, he took a packet of cigarettes from his pocket. But after his first glance at the child's face he put it back.

From his chair Castel looked at Rieux, over his spectacles.

'Any news of his father?'

'No. He's in the Isolation Camp.'

The doctor's hands were gripping the rail of the bed, his eyes fixed on the small tortured body. Suddenly it stiffened, and seemed to give a little at the waist, as slowly the arms and legs spread out X-wise. From the body, naked under an army blanket, rose a smell of damp wool and stale sweat. The boy had gritted his teeth again. Then very gradually he relaxed, bringing his arms and legs back towards the centre of the bed, still without speaking or opening his eyes, and his breathing seemed to quicken. Rieux looked at Tarrou, who hastily lowered his eyes.

They had already seen children die—for many months now death had shown no favouritism—but they had never yet watched a child's agony minute by minute, as they had now been doing since daybreak. Needless to say, the pain inflicted on these innocent victims had always seemed to them to be what in fact it was: an abominable thing. But hitherto they had felt its abomination in, so to speak, an abstract way; they had never had to witness over so long a period the death-throes of an innocent child.

And, just then, the boy had a sudden spasm, as if something had bitten him in the stomach, and uttered a long, shrill wail. For moments that seemed endless he stayed in a queer, contorted position, his body racked by convulsive tremors; it was as if his frail frame were bending before the fierce breath of the plague, breaking under the reiterated gusts of fever. Then the storm-wind passed, there came a lull, and he relaxed a little; the fever seemed to recede, leaving him gasping for breath on a dank, pestilential shore, lost in a languor that already looked like death. When for the third time the fiery wave broke on him, lifting him a little, the child curled himself up and shrank away to the edge of the bed, as if in terror of the flames advancing on him, licking his limbs. A moment later, after tossing his head wildly to and fro, he flung off the blanket. From between the inflamed eyelids big tears welled up and trickled down the sunken, leaden-hued cheeks. When the spasm had passed, utterly exhausted, tensing his thin legs and arms on which, within forty-eight hours, the flesh had wasted to the bone, the child lay flat, racked on the tumbled bed, in a grotesque parody of crucifixion.

Bending, Tarrou gently stroked with his big paw the small face stained with tears and sweat. Castel had closed his book a few moments before, and his eyes were now fixed on the child. He begun to speak, but had to give a cough before continuing, because his voice rang out so harshly.

'There wasn't any remission this morning, was there, Rieux?'

Rieux shook his head, adding, however, that the child was putting up more resistance than one would have expected. Paneloux, who was slumped against the wall, said in a low voice:

'So, if he is to die, he will have suffered longer.'

Light was increasing in the ward. The occupants of the other nine beds were tossing about and groaning, but in tones that seemed deliberately subdued. Only one—at the far end of the ward—was screaming, or, rather, uttering little exclamations at regular intervals, which seemed to convey surprise more than pain. Indeed one had the impression that even for the sufferers the frantic terror of the early phase had passed, and there was a sort of mournful resignation in their present attitude towards the disease. Only the child went on fighting with all his little might. Now and again Rieux took his pulse—less because this served any purpose than as an escape from his utter helplessness—and, when he closed his eyes, he seemed to feel its tumult, mingling with the fever of his own blood. And then, at one with the tortured child, he struggled to sustain him with all the remaining strength of his own body. But linked for a few moments, the rhythms of their heart-beats soon fell apart, the child escaped him, and again he knew his impotence. Then he released the small, thin wrist and moved back to his place.

The light on the whitewashed walls was changing from pink to yellow. The first waves of another day of heat were beating on the windows. They hardly heard Grand saying he would come back, as he turned to go. All were waiting. The child, his eyes still closed, seemed to grow a little calmer. His clawlike fingers were feebly plucking at the sides of the bed. Then they rose, scratched at the blanket over his knees, and suddenly he doubled up his limbs, bringing his thighs above his stomach, and remained quite still. For the first time he opened his eyes, and gazed at Rieux, who was standing immediately in front of him. In the small face, rigid as a mask of greyish clay, slowly the lips parted and from them rose a long, incessant scream, hardly varying with his respiration, and filling the ward with a fierce, indignant protest, so little childish that it seemed like a collective voice issuing from all the sufferers there. Rieux clenched his jaws, Tarrou looked away. Rambert went and stood beside Castel, whose closed book was lying on his knees. Paneloux gazed down at the small mouth, fouled with the sordes of the plague and pouring out the angry death-cry that has sounded through the ages of mankind. He sank on to his knees, and all present found it natural to hear him say in a voice hoarse but clearly audible across that nameless, never-ending wail:

'My God, spare this child . . .!'

But the wail continued without cease and the other sufferers began to grow restless. The patient at the far end of the ward, whose little broken cries had gone on without a break, now quickened their tempo so that they flowed together in one unbroken cry, while the others' groans grew louder. A gust of sobs swept through the room, drowning Paneloux's prayer, and Rieux, who was still tightly gripping the rail of the bed, shut his eyes, dazed with exhaustion and disgust.

When he opened them again, Tarrou was at his side.

'I must go,' Rieux said. 'I can't bear to hear them any longer.'

But then, suddenly, the other sufferers fell silent. And now the doctor grew aware that the child's wail, after weakening more and more, had fluttered out into silence. Round him the groans began again, but more faintly, like a far echo of the fight that now was over. For it was over. Castel had moved round to the other side of the bed and said the end had come. His mouth still gaping, but silent now, the child was lying amongst the tumbled blankets, a small, shrunken form, with the tears still wet on his cheeks.

Paneloux went up to the bed, and made the sign of benediction. Then gathering up his cassock, he walked out by the passage between the beds.

'Will you have to start it all over again?' Tarrou asked Castel.

The old doctor nodded slowly, with a twisted smile.

'Perhaps. After all, he put up a surprisingly long resistance.'

Rieux was already on his way out, walking so quickly and with such a strange look on his face that Paneloux put out an arm to check him when he was about to pass him in the doorway.

'Come, doctor . . .' he began.

Rieux swung round on him fiercely.

'Ah! That child, anyhow, was innocent—and you know it as well as I do!'

He strode on, brushing past Paneloux, and walked across the school playground. Sitting on a wooden bench under the dingy, stunted trees, he wiped off the sweat which was beginning to run into his eyes. He felt like shouting imprecations—anything to loosen the stranglehold lashing his heart with steel! Heat was flooding down between the branches of the fig trees. A white haze, spreading rapidly over the blue of the morning sky, made the air yet more stifling. Rieux lay back wearily on the bench. Gazing up at the ragged branches, the shimmering sky, he slowly got back his breath and fought down his fatigue.

He heard a voice behind him.

'Why was there that anger in your voice just now? What we'd been seeing was as unbearable to me as it was to you.'

Rieux turned towards Paneloux.

'I know. I'm sorry. But weariness is a kind of madness. And there are times when the only feeling I have is one of mad revolt.'

'I understand,' Paneloux said in a low voice. 'That sort of thing is revolting because it passes our human understanding. But perhaps we should love what we cannot understand.'

Rieux straightened up slowly. He gazed at Paneloux, summoning to his gaze all the strength and fervour he could muster against his weariness. Then he shook his head.

'No, Father. I've a very different idea of love. And until my dying day I shall refuse to love a scheme of things in which children are put to torture.'

A shade of disquietude crossed the priest's face. He was silent for a moment. Then, 'Ah, doctor,' he said sadly, 'I've just realized what is meant by "grace".'

Rieux had sunk back again on the bench. His lassitude had returned and from its depths he spoke, more gently.

'It's something I haven't got; that I know. But I'd rather not discuss that with you. We're working side by side for something that unites us—beyond blasphemy and prayers. And it's the only thing that matters.'

Paneloux sat down beside Rieux. It was obvious that he was deeply moved.

'Yes, yes,' he said, 'you, too, are working for man's salvation.'

Rieux tried to smile.

'Salvation's much too big a word for me. I don't aim so high. I'm concerned with man's health; and for me his health comes first.'

Paneloux seemed to hesitate. 'Doctor ...' he began, then fell silent. Down his face, too, sweat was trickling. Murmuring, 'Goodbye for the present,' he rose. His eyes were moist. When he turned to go, Rieux, who had seemed lost in thought, suddenly rose and took a step towards him.

'Again, please forgive me. I can promise there won't be another outburst of that kind.'

Paneloux held out his hand, saying regretfully:

'And yet—I haven't convinced you!'

'What does it matter? What I hate is death and disease—as you well know. And whether you wish it or not, we're allies, facing them and fighting them together.' Rieux was still holding Paneloux's hand. 'So you see—' but he refrained from meeting the priest's eyes—'God Himself can't part us now.'

POINTS FOR DISCUSSION

1. What distinguishes this passage from other death-bed scenes you may have read? Consider what Camus's motives are in writing such a passage. Would it have been as effective (in whatever sense you like) if he had described the death of an adult and not of a child?

2. Is it a peculiarly modern view to be so outraged by the sight of death and suffering?

3. Summarize the different reactions of Rieux and Paneloux to the problem of pain and suffering as exemplified in the death of this small child.

4. What do you think Rieux means when he says, 'God Himself can't part us now'?

5. Is it possible to get a warped view of the problem of pain by being too concerned with one's *own* feelings when contemplating the sufferings of others?

6. In another sermon, after the death of M. Othon's child, Paneloux said that we must believe everything or deny everything; it was wrong to say, '*This* I understand but *that* I cannot accept.' We must go straight to the heart of that which is unacceptable, precisely because is it is thus that we are constrained to make our choice. Do you agree with Paneloux that it is in this 'confrontation with the unacceptable' that the only true decision about one's faith can be made?

2. ALDOUS HUXLEY

BRAVE NEW WORLD

ALDOUS HUXLEY (1894–1963) was educated at Eton and at Balliol College, Oxford. His ability as a trenchant and witty critic of various aspects of modern society was shown in his earlier novels such as *Crome Yellow* (1921) and *Antic Hay* (1923), in which he satirized the philistinism, phoneyness, and materialism of post-war Britain. In *Brave New World*, which was published in 1932, the object of his attack is the excessive optimism about the effects which scientific progress may have upon human individuality, and in it he describes the sort of life which he imagines could be produced in years to come by developments in the sciences of biology, physiology, and psychology; for in Huxley's opinion it was by these 'sciences of life' rather than by the 'sciences of matter' that the essential quality of our life was most likely to be changed.

Brave New World opens in the Central London Hatchery and Conditioning Centre where the Director is explaining the mysteries of his laboratory to some new students. There is, of course, no such thing as normal birth in the Brave New World; the very idea of parenthood is obscene. Instead, people are produced from incubators; one ovary can be so divided as to produce several thousands of identical human beings, who at various stages of their development are so treated as to emerge in carefully defined grades of ability, ranging from Epsilons (who do all the menial work) through Deltas, Gammas, and Betas to Alphas. After 'birth', all are conditioned. As the Director says, 'that is the secret of happiness and virtue—liking what you've *got* to do. All conditioning aims at that; making people like their unescapable social destiny.'

In this community, violent human emotions are thought to be a threat to stability, and therefore a passion such as love cannot be tolerated; but there is plenty of sex—but for pleasure only, and not as a means of procreation; to produce a child by mistake is regarded as calamitous. The greatest source of pleasure is the release given by a drug called 'soma'. One of the leading inhabitants sums up the Brave New World as follows:

> People are happy; they get what they want, and they never want what they can't get. They're well off; they're safe; they're never ill; they're not afraid of death; they're blissfully ignorant of passion and old age; they're plagued with no mothers or fathers; they've got no wives, or children or loves to feel strongly about; they're so con-

ditioned that they practically can't help behaving as they ought to behave. And if anything should go wrong, there's soma.

There are ten World Controllers, one of whom, Mustapha Mond, is the Controller for western Europe. Not all the world, however, lies within the borders of the Brave New World; there are still a few areas outside, called 'reservations', where the 'savages' live. The savages of course still live, grow old, and die in all the unstable mixture of misery and joy that is part of human life as we know it.

This then is the setting in which the story takes place. Bernard Marx, an alpha-plus psychologist, and his current girl-friend Lenina visit the New Mexico Reservation in order to see the savages. While they are there, they are astonished to meet a young, white-skinned man who speaks English. It emerges that several years earlier Linda, his mother, and the Director of the Hatchery Centre had visited this reservation on a similar holiday; Linda had carelessly let herself become pregnant and then had been conveniently lost and left behind. She had brought up her son among the Indians, his sole sources of education being his mother's nostalgic reminiscences of life in the Brave New World and, oddly, a volume of Shakespeare. Linda, who has aged naturally and therefore seems utterly repulsive to the visitors, and her son John are taken back to the Brave New World as objects of scientific interest.

John, unconditioned to his new surroundings, falls deeply in love with Lenina (which is something she cannot understand at all) and soon develops a loathing for this Utopia. The turning point comes when his mother dies in the artificial cheeriness of the Park Lane Hospital for the Dying, where no human grief is expected or catered for, and John breaks out into open rebellion and violence. After an interview with Mustapha Mond, which is recounted in the extracts below, the Savage rejects the Brave New World and goes to live in a deserted air-light-house near Guildford, where as the 'Savage of Surrey' he becomes an object of interest for sightseers and finally hangs himself.

(a) Mustapha Mond explains that God is not compatible with universal happiness

'Art, science—you seem to have paid a fairly high price for your happiness,' said the Savage, when they were alone. 'Anything else?'

'Well, religion, of course,' replied the Controller. 'There used to be something called God—before the Nine Years' War. But I was forgetting; you know all about God, I suppose.'

'Well . . .' The Savage hesitated. He would have liked to say something about solitude, about night, about the mesa lying pale under the moon, about the precipice, the plunge into shadowy darkness, about death. He would have liked to speak; but there were no words. Not even in Shakespeare.

The Controller, meanwhile, had crossed to the other side of the room and was unlocking a large safe let into the wall between the bookshelves. The heavy door swung open. Rummaging in the darkness within, 'It's a subject', he said, 'that has always had a great interest for me.' He pulled out a thick black volume. 'You've never read this, for example.'

The Savage took it. '*The Holy Bible, containing the Old and New Testaments*,' he read aloud from the title-page.

'Nor this.' It was a small book and had lost its cover.

'*The Imitation of Christ.*'

'Nor this.' He handed out another volume.

'*The Varieties of Religious Experience*. By William James.'

'And I've got plenty more,' Mustapha Mond continued, resuming his seat. 'A whole collection of pornographic old books. God in the safe and Ford on the shelves.' He pointed with a laugh to his avowed library—to the shelves of books, the racks full of reading-machine bobbins and sound-track rolls.

'But if you know about God, why don't you tell them?' asked the Savage indignantly. 'Why don't you give them these books about God?'

'For the same reason as we don't give them *Othello*: they're old; they're about God hundreds of years ago. Not about God now.'

'But God doesn't change.'

'Men do, though.'

'What difference does that make?'

'All the difference in the world,' said Mustapha Mond. He got up again and walked to the safe. 'There was a man called Cardinal Newman,' he said. 'A cardinal', he exclaimed paren-thetically, 'was a kind of Arch-Community-Songster.'

' "I, Pandulph, of fair Milan cardinal." I've read about them in Shakespeare.'

'Of course you have. Well, as I was saying, there was a man called Cardinal Newman. Ah, here's the book.' He pulled it out.

'And while I'm about it I'll take this one too. It's by a man called Maine de Biran. He was a philosopher, if you know what that was.'

'A man who dreams of fewer things than there are in heaven and earth,' said the Savage promptly.

'Quite so. I'll read you one of the things that he *did* dream of in a moment. Meanwhile, listen to what this old Arch-Community-Songster said.' He opened the book at the place marked by a slip of paper and began to read. ' "We are not our own any more than what we possess is our own. We did not make ourselves, we cannot be supreme over ourselves. We are not our own masters. We are God's property. Is it not our happiness thus to view the matter? Is it any happiness, or any comfort, to consider that we *are* our own? It may be thought so by the young and prosperous. These may think it a great thing to have everything, as they suppose, their own way—to depend on no one—to have to think of nothing out of sight, to be without the irksomeness of continual acknowledgement, continual prayer, continual reference of what they do to the will of another. But as time goes on, they, as all men, will find that independence was not made for man—that it is an unnatural state—will do for a while, but will not carry us on safely to the end . . ." ' Mustapha Mond paused, put down the first book and, picking up the other, turned over the pages. 'Take this, for example,' he said, and in his deep voice once more began to read: ' "A man grows old; he feels in himself that radical sense of weakness, of listlessness, of discomfort, which accompanies the advance of age; and, feeling thus, imagines himself merely sick, lulling his fears with the notion that this distressing condition is due to some particular cause, from which, as from an illness, he hopes to recover. Vain imaginings! That sickness is old age; and a horrible disease it is. They say that it is the fear of death and of what comes after death that makes men turn to religion as they advance in years. But my own experience has given me the conviction that, quite apart from any such terrors or imaginings, the religious sentiment tends to develop as we grow older; to develop because, as the passions grow calm, as the fancy and sensibilities are less excited and less excitable, our reason becomes less troubled in its working, less obscured by the images, desires and distractions, in which it used to be absorbed; whereupon God emerges as from behind a cloud; our soul feels, sees, turns towards the source of all light; turns naturally and inevitably; for now that

all that gave to the world of sensations its life and charm has
begun to leak away from us, now that phenomenal existence is no
more bolstered up by impressions from within or from without,
we feel the need to lean on something that abides, something that
will never play us false—a reality, an absolute and everlasting
truth. Yes, we inevitably turn to God; for this religious sentiment
is of its nature so pure, so delightful to the soul that experiences it,
that it makes up to us for all our other losses." ' Mustapha Mond
shut the book and leaned back in his chair. 'One of the numerous
things in heaven and earth that these philosophers didn't dream
about was this' (he waved his hand), 'us, the modern world. "You
can only be independent of God while you've got youth and prosperity; independence won't take you safely to the end." Well,
we've now got youth and prosperity right up to the end. What
follows? Evidently, that we can be independent of God. "The religious sentiment will compensate us for all our losses." But there
aren't any losses for us to compensate; religious sentiment is
superfluous. And why should we go hunting for a substitute for
youthful desires, when youthful desires never fail? A substitute for
distractions, when we go on enjoying all the old fooleries to
the very last? What need have we of repose when our minds and
bodies continue to delight in activity? of consolation, when we
have *soma*? of something immovable, when there is the social
order?'

'Then you think there is no God?'

'No, I think there quite probably is one.'

'Then why . . .?'

Mustapha Mond checked him. 'But he manifests himself in
different ways to different men. In pre-modern times he mani-
fested himself as the being that's described in these books.
Now . . .'

'How does he manifest himself now?' asked the Savage.

'Well, he manifests himself as an absence; as though he weren't
there at all.'

'That's your fault.'

'Call it the fault of civilization. God isn't compatible with
machinery and scientific medicine and universal happiness. You
must make your choice. Our civilization has chosen machinery
and medicine and happiness. That's why I have to keep these
books locked up in the safe. They're smut. People would be
shocked if . . .'

The Savage interrupted him. 'But isn't it *natural* to feel there's a God?'.

'You might as well ask if it's natural to do up one's trousers with zippers,' said the Controller sarcastically. 'You remind me of another of those old fellows called Bradley. He defined philosophy as the finding of bad reasons for what one believes by instinct. As if one believed anything by instinct! One believes things because one has been conditioned to believe them. Finding bad reasons for what one believes for other bad reasons—that's philosophy. People believe in God because they've been conditioned to believe in God.'

'But all the same,' insisted the Savage, 'it is natural to believe in God when you're alone—quite alone, in the night, thinking about death . . .'

'But people never are alone now,' said Mustapha Mond. 'We make them hate solitude; and we arrange their lives so that it's almost impossible for them ever to have it.'

The Savage nodded gloomily. At Malpais he had suffered because they had shut him out from the communal activities of the pueblo, in civilized London he was suffering because he could never escape from those communal activities, never be quietly alone.

POINTS FOR DISCUSSION

1. Mustapha Mond considers that religion is merely 'a substitute for youthful desires'. What do you think of this view? To what extent is he supported by the religious writers whom he quotes?

2. 'God isn't compatible with machinery and scientific medicine and universal happiness.' Is there any evidence that progress in science and technology will eventually make the concept of God superfluous?

3. 'One believes things because one has been conditioned to believe them.' Discuss what is meant by the word 'conditioned' here. How does it differ from the word 'educated'? Do you agree with Mustapha Mond's remark?

4. 'But all the same,' insisted the Savage, 'it is natural to believe in God when you're alone—quite alone, in the night, thinking about death . . .' What do you think of this line of thought? How do you think the Savage might have developed this argument if he had been given the chance?

5. Suggest some reasons why the Brave New World hated solitude.

(b) The Savage claims the right to be unhappy

'Come, come,' protested Mustapha Mond, 'that's going rather far isn't it?'

'If you allowed yourselves to think of God, you wouldn't allow yourselves to be degraded by pleasant vices. You'd have a reason for bearing things patiently, for doing things with courage. I've seen it with the Indians.'

'I'm sure you have,' said Mustapha Mond. 'But then we aren't Indians. There isn't any need for a civilized man to bear anything that's seriously unpleasant. And as for doing things—Ford forbid that he should get the idea into his head. It would upset the whole social order if men started doing things on their own.'

'What about self-denial, then? If you had a God, you'd have a reason for self-denial.'

'But industrial civilization is only possible when there's no self-denial. Self-indulgence up to the very limits imposed by hygiene and economics. Otherwise the wheels stop turning.'

'You'd have a reason for chastity!' said the Savage, blushing a little as he spoke the words.

'But chastity means passion, chastity means neurasthenia. And passion and neurasthenia mean instability. And instability means the end of civilization. You can't have a lasting civilization without plenty of pleasant vices.'

'But God's the reason for everything noble and fine and heroic. If you had a God . . .'

'My dear young friend,' said Mustapha Mond, 'civilization has absolutely no need of nobility or heroism. These things are symptoms of political inefficiency. In a properly organized society like ours, nobody has any opportunities for being noble or heroic. Conditions have got to be thoroughly unstable before the occasion can arise. Where there are wars, where there are divided allegiances, where there are temptations to be resisted, objects of love to be fought for or defended—there, obviously, nobility and heroism have some sense. But there aren't any wars nowadays. The greatest care is taken to prevent you from loving anyone too much. There's no such thing as a divided allegiance; you're so conditioned that you can't help doing what you ought to do. And what you ought to do is on the whole so pleasant, so many of the natural impulses are allowed free play, that there really aren't any temptations to resist. And if ever, by some unlucky chance, anything unpleasant should somehow happen, why, there's always *soma* to give you a holiday from the facts. And there's always *soma* to calm your anger, to reconcile you to your enemies, to make you patient and long-suffering. In the past you could only accomplish these things by making a great effort and after years of hard moral training. Now, you swallow two or three half-gramme tablets, and there you are. Anybody can be virtuous now. You can carry at least half your morality about in a bottle. Christianity without tears—that's what *soma* is.'

'But the tears are necessary. Don't you remember what Othello said? "If after every tempest come such calms, may the winds blow till they have wakened death." There's a story one of the old Indians used to tell us, about the Girl of Mátsaki. The young men who wanted to marry her had to do a morning's hoeing in her garden. It seemed easy; but there were flies and mosquitoes, magic ones. Most of the young men simply couldn't stand the biting and stinging. But the one that could—he got the girl.'

'Charming! But in civilized countries,' said the Controller, 'you can have girls without hoeing for them; and there aren't any flies or mosquitoes to sting you. We got rid of them all centuries ago.'

The Savage nodded, frowning. 'You got rid of them. Yes, that's just like you. Getting rid of everything unpleasant instead of learning to put up with it. Whether 'tis nobler in the mind to suffer the slings and arrows of outrageous fortune, or to take arms against a sea of troubles and by opposing end them. . . . But you don't do either. Neither suffer nor oppose. You just abolish the slings and arrows. It's too easy.'

He was suddenly silent, thinking of his mother. In her room on the thirty-seventh floor, Linda had floated in a sea of singing lights and perfumed caresses—floated away, out of space, out of time, out of the prison of her memories, her habits, her aged and bloated body. And Tomakin, ex-Director of Hatcheries and Conditioning, Tomakin was still on holiday—on holiday from humiliation and pain, in a world where he could not hear those words, that derisive laughter, could not see that hideous face, feel those moist and flabby arms round his neck, in a beautiful world . . .

'What you need', the Savage went on, 'is something *with* tears for a change. Nothing costs enough here.'

('Twelve and a half million dollars,' Henry Foster had protested when the Savage told him that. 'Twelve and a half million —that's what the new Conditioning Centre cost. Not a cent less.')

'Exposing what is mortal and unsure to all that fortune, death and danger dare, even for an egg-shell. Isn't there something in that?' he asked, looking up at Mustapha Mond. 'Quite apart from God—though of course God would be a reason for it. Isn't there something in living dangerously?'

'There's a great deal in it,' the Controller replied. 'Men and women must have their adrenals stimulated from time to time.'

'What?' questioned the Savage, uncomprehending.

'It's one of the conditions of perfect health. That's why we've made the V.P.S. treatments compulsory.'

'V.P.S.?'

'Violent Passion Surrogate. Regularly once a month. We flood the whole system with adrenalin. It's the complete physiological equivalent of fear and rage. All the tonic effects of murdering Desdemona and being murdered by Othello, without any of the inconveniences.'

'But I like the inconveniences.'

'We don't,' said the Controller. 'We prefer to do things comfortably.'

'But I don't want comfort. I want God, I want poetry, I want real danger, I want freedom, I want goodness. I want sin.'

'In fact,' said Mustapha Mond, 'you're claiming the right to be unhappy.'

'All right, then,' said the Savage defiantly, 'I'm claiming the right to be unhappy.'

'Not to mention the right to grow old and ugly and impotent; the right to have syphilis and cancer; the right to have too little to eat; the right to be lousy; the right to live in constant apprehension of what may happen tomorrow; the right to catch typhoid; the right to be tortured by unspeakable pains of every kind.'

There was a long silence.

'I claim them all,' said the Savage at last.

Mustapha Mond shrugged his shoulders. 'You're welcome,' he said.

POINTS FOR DISCUSSION

1. What criticisms does Huxley here seem to be making of twentieth century civilization?

2. Why does the Savage make such a paradoxical demand as 'I claim the right to be unhappy'?

3. In a foreword to a later edition Huxley says that a serious defect of the book is that the Savage is offered only two choices, 'an insane life in Utopia or the life of a primitive Indian village, a life more human in some respects but in others hardly less queer and abnormal'. If he were to re-write the book, he would, he says, give the Savage a third choice. What do you think he had in mind?

4. Consider the Savage's remark, 'I want God, I want poetry, I want real danger, I want freedom, I want goodness. I want sin.' Does this remark seem to you to spring from some profound truth? Or do you think that it merely springs out of a surfeit of material comforts?

3. EUGENE IONESCO

RHINOCEROS

EUGENE IONESCO, one of the most important writers of the Theatre of the Absurd (see page 55) was born in Rumania in 1912. His mother was French, and soon after his birth his parents moved to Paris. Later on the family went back to Rumania and Ionesco studied French at the University in Bucharest. He returned to France in 1938 to work on a thesis.

Ionesco's first play, *The Bald Prima Donna*, was not written until 1948 and must surely be the only play which owes its inspiration to the inanities of the conversation between two 'characters' (Mr. and Mrs. Smith) in an elementary textbook for learning English. The whole play consists of an evening's inconsequential and eventually utterly incoherent chatter between Mr. and Mrs. Smith and their friends, and is intended as a comment on the 'absurdity of the commonplace' and the way in which sheer conformity can turn people into automata and can destroy their individuality. One of his most controversial plays is *The Chairs*, in which a long-awaited message of the greatest importance turns out to be horrifyingly inarticulate mumblings mouthed at an audience consisting entirely of chairs. These two plays illustrate some recurrent themes in Ionesco's writings—the artificiality and boredom of much of modern western civilization, and the feeling of futility which results from the loss of a deeply-felt belief about the meaning of life.

In spite of the seriousness of their themes, Ionesco's plays are full of humour, as the following extract from *Rhinoceros* will illustrate. The leading character is Bérenger, who appears in several of his plays. One morning in the small provincial town where Bérenger lives, a rhinoceros is seen running up the main street; later on another rhinoceros is seen, and then more and more. As the numbers increase and their antics become more and more extraordinary, it becomes clear that the inhabitants are infected with a strange disease, 'rhinoceritis', which makes them want to turn into these creatures—and gradually they do so. Eventually Bérenger is the only man who resists the disease, and as the play ends he is left alone on the stage shouting out his refusal to capitulate.

The play is clearly a satire on the self-destructive conformity that threatens human individuality. What precisely are the pressures that threaten us Ionesco does not specify; but in an interview in *Le Monde* he once said:

People allow themselves suddenly to be invaded by a new religion, a doctrine, a fanaticism. . . . At such moments we witness a veritable mental mutation. I don't know if you have noticed it, but when people no longer share your opinions, when you can no longer make yourself understood by them, one has the impression of being confronted by monsters—rhinoceroses, for example. They have that mixture of candour and ferocity. . . .

Most of the play is extremely funny; but what is illuminating is the variety of reasons that Bérenger's friends give for joining the rhinoceroses, as is shown in the extracts below, both of which should be read before attempting the points for discussion.

(a) Bérenger visits his friend Jean and is alarmed to find him already in the process of becoming a rhinoceros

BERENGER [looking fixedly at Jean]: Do you know what's happened to Boeuf? He's turned into a rhinoceros.

JEAN: What happened to Boeuf?

BERENGER: He's turned into a rhinoceros.

JEAN [fanning himself with the flaps of his jacket]: Brrr . . .

BERENGER: Come on now, stop joking.

JEAN: I can puff if I want to, can't I? I've every right . . . I'm in my own house.

BERENGER: I didn't say you couldn't.

JEAN: And I shouldn't if I were you. I feel hot, I feel hot. Brrr . . . Just a moment. I must cool myself down.

BERENGER [whilst JEAN darts to the bathroom]: He must have a fever.

[JEAN is in the bathroom, one hears him puffing, and also the sound of a running tap.]

JEAN [off]: Brrr . . .

BERENGER: He's got the shivers. I'm jolly well going to phone the doctor. [He goes to the telephone again then comes back quickly when he hears Jean's voice.]

JEAN [off]: So old Boeuf turned into a rhinoceros, did he? Ah, ah, ah . . .! He was just having you on, he'd disguised himself. [He pokes his head round the bathroom door. He is very green. The bump over his nose is slightly larger.] He was just disguised.

BERENGER [*walking about the room, without seeing Jean*]: He looked very serious about it, I assure you.

JEAN: Oh well, that's his business.

BERENGER [*turning to Jean who disappears again into the bathroom*]: I'm sure he didn't do it on purpose. He didn't want to change.

JEAN [*off*]: How do you know?

BERENGER: Well, everything led one to suppose so.

JEAN: And what if he did do it on purpose? Eh? What if he did it on purpose?

BERENGER: I'd be very surprised. At any rate, Mrs. Boeuf didn't seem to know about it ...

JEAN [*in a very hoarse voice*]: Ah, ah, ah! Fat old Mrs. Boeuf. She's just a fool!

BERENGER: Well fool or no fool ...

JEAN [*he enters swiftly, takes off his jacket, and throws it on the bed.* BERENGER *discreetly averts his gaze.* JEAN, *whose back and chest are now green, goes back into the bathroom. As he walks in and out*]: Boeuff never let his wife know what he was up to ...

BERENGER: You're wrong there, Jean—it was a very united family.

JEAN: Very united, was it? Are you sure? Hum, hum. Brrr ...

BERENGER [*moving to the bathroom, where Jean slams the door in his face*]: Very united. And the proof is that ...

JEAN [*from within*]: Boeuf led his own private life. He had a secret side to him deep down which he kept to himself.

BERENGER: I shouldn't make you talk, it seems to upset you.

JEAN: On the contrary, it relaxes me.

BERENGER: Even so, let me call the doctor, I beg you.

JEAN: I absolutely forbid it. I can't stand obstinate people.

[JEAN *comes back into the bedroom.* BERENGER *backs away a little scared, for* JEAN *is greener than ever and speaks only with difficulty. His voice is unrecognizable.*]

Well, whether he changes into a rhinoceros on purpose or against his will, he's probably all the better for it.

BERENGER: How can you say a thing like that? Surely you don't think ...

JEAN: You always see the black side of everything. It obviously gave him great pleasure to turn into a rhinoceros. There's nothing extraordinary in that.

BERENGER: There's nothing extraordinary in it, but I doubt if it gave him much pleasure.

JEAN: And why not, pray?

BERENGER: It's hard to say exactly why; it's just something you feel.

JEAN: I tell you it's not as bad as all that. After all, rhinoceroses are living creatures the same as us; they've got as much right to life as we have!

BERENGER: As long as they don't destroy ours in the process. You must admit the difference in mentality.

JEAN [pacing up and down the room, and in and out of the bath-room]: Are you under the impression that our way of life is superior?

BERENGER: Well at any rate, we have our own moral standards which I consider incompatible with the standards of these animals.

JEAN: Moral standards! I'm sick of moral standards! We need to go beyond moral standards!

BERENGER: What would you put in their place?

JEAN [still pacing]: Nature!

BERENGER: Nature?

JEAN: Nature has its own laws. Morality's against Nature.

BERENGER: Are you suggesting we replace our moral laws by the law of the jungle?

JEAN: It would suit me, suit me fine.

BERENGER: You say that. But deep down, no one ...

JEAN [interrupting him, pacing up and down]: We've got to build our life on new foundations. We must get back to primeval integrity.

BERENGER: I don't agree with you at all.

JEAN [breathing noisily]: I can't breathe.

BERENGER: Just think a moment. You must admit that we have a philosophy that animals don't share, and an irreplaceable set of values, which it's taken centuries of human civilization to build up ...

JEAN [in the bathroom]: When we've demolished all that, we'll be better off!

BERENGER: I know you don't mean that seriously. You're joking! It's just a poetic fancy.

JEAN: Brrr. [He almost trumpets.]

BERENGER: I'd never realized you were a poet.

JEAN [*comes out of the bathroom*]: Brrr. [*He trumpets again.*]

BERENGER: That's not what you believe fundamentally—I know you too well. You know as well as I do that mankind . . .

JEAN [*interrupting him*]: Don't talk to me about mankind!

BERENGER: I mean the human individual, humanism . . .

JEAN: Humanism is all washed up! You're a ridiculous old senti- mentalist. [*He goes into the bathroom.*]

BERENGER: But you must admit that the mind . . .

JEAN [*from the bathroom*]: Just clichés! You talking rubbish!

BERENGER: Rubbish!

JEAN [*from the bathroom in a very hoarse voice, difficult to under- stand*]: Utter rubbish!

BERENGER: I'm amazed to hear you say that, Jean, really! You must be out of your mind. You wouldn't like to be a rhinoceros yourself, now would you?

JEAN: Why not? I'm not a victim of prejudice like you.

BERENGER: Can you speak more clearly? I didn't catch what you said. You swallowed the words.

JEAN [*still in the bathroom*]: Then keep your ears open.

BERENGER: What?

JEAN: Keep your ears open. I said what's wrong with being a rhinoceros? I'm all for change.

BERENGER: It's not like you to say a thing like that . . .

[BERENGER *stops short, for* JEAN'S *appearance is truly alarm- ing. Jean has become, in fact, completely green. The bump on his forehead is practically a rhinoceros horn.*]

Oh! You really must be out of your mind!

(b) *Dudard, a friend of Bérenger and a promising young official in the Department where they both work, tells Bérenger of the 'rhinoceritis' of Mr Papillon, the head of the Department. Dudard eventually joins the rhinoceroses in order to criticize them 'from the inside'*

DUDARD: I suppose I might as well tell you . . . it's really rather funny—the fact is, he turned into a rhinoceros.

[*Distant rhinoceros noises.*]

BERENGER: A rhinoceros ! ! ! Mr Papillon a rhinoceros! I can't believe it! I don't think it's funny at all! Why didn't you tell me before?

DUDARD: Well, you know you've no sense of humour. I didn't want to tell you ... I didn't want to tell you because I knew very well you wouldn't see the funny side, and it would upset you. You know how impressionable you are!

BERENGER [raising his arms to heaven]: Oh that's awful ... Mr Papillon! And he had such a good job.

DUDARD: That proves his metamorphosis was sincere.

BERENGER: He couldn't have done it on purpose. I'm certain it must have been involuntary.

DUDARD: How can we tell? It's hard to know the real reasons for people's decisions.

BERENGER: He must have made a mistake. He'd got some hidden complexes. He should have been psychoanalysed.

DUDARD: Even if it's a case of dissociation it's still very revealing. It was his way of sublimating himself.

BERENGER: He let himself be talked into it, I feel sure.

DUDARD: That could happen to anybody!

BERENGER [alarmed]: To anybody? Oh no, not to you it couldn't —could it? And not to me!

DUDARD: We must hope not.

BERENGER: Because we don't want to ... that's so, isn't it? Tell me, that is so, isn't it?

DUDARD: Yes, yes, of course ...

BERENGER [a little calmer]: I still would have thought Mr Papillon would have had the strength to resist. I thought he had a bit more character! Particularly as I fail to see where his interest lay—what possible material or moral interest ...

DUDARD: It was obviously a disinterested gesture on his part.

BERENGER: Obviously. There were extenuating circumstances ... or were they aggravating? Aggravating, I should think, because if he did it from choice ... You know I feel sure that Botard must have taken a very poor view of it—what did he think of his Chief's behaviour?

DUDARD: Oh poor old Botard was quite indignant, absolutely outraged. I've rarely seen anyone so incensed.

BERENGER: Well, for once I'm on his side. He's a good man after all. A man of sound common sense. And to think I misjudged him.

DUDARD: He misjudged you, too.

BERENGER: That proves how objective I'm being now. Besides, you had a pretty bad opinion of him yourself.

DUDARD: I wouldn't say I had a bad opinion. I admit I didn't often agree with him. I never liked his scepticism, the way he was always so incredulous and suspicious. Even in this instance I didn't approve of him entirely.

BERENGER: This time for the opposite reasons.

DUDARD: No, not exactly—my own reasoning and my judgement are a bit more complex than you seem to think. It was because there was nothing precise or objective about the way Botard argued. I don't approve of the rhinoceroses myself, as you know—not at all, don't go thinking that! But Botard's attitude was too passionate, as usual, and therefore over-simplified. His stand seems to me entirely dictated by hatred of his superiors. That's where he gets his inferiority complex and his resentment. What's more he talks in clichés, and commonplace arguments leave me cold.

BERENGER: Well, forgive me, but this time I'm in complete agreement with Botard. He's somebody worthwhile.

DUDARD: I don't deny it, but that doesn't meant anything.

BERENGER: He's a very worthwhile person—and they're not easy to find these days. He's down-to-earth, with four feet planted firmly on the ground—I mean, both feet. I'm in complete agreement with him, and I'm proud of it. I shall congratulate him when I see him. I deplore Mr Papillon's action; it was his duty not to succumb.

DUDARD: How intolerant you are! Maybe Papillon felt the need for a bit of relaxation after all these years of office life.

BERENGER [*ironically*]: And you're too tolerant, far too broad-minded!

DUDARD: My dear Berenger, one must always make an effort to understand. And in order to understand a phenomenon and its effects you need to work back to the initial causes, by honest intellectual effort. We must try to do this because, after all, we are thinking beings. I haven't yet succeeded, as I told you, and I don't know if I shall succeed. But in any case one has to start out favourably disposed—or at least, impartial; one has to keep an open mind—that's essential to a scientific mentality. Everything is logical. To understand is to justify.

BERENGER: You'll be siding with the rhinoceroses before long.

DUDARD: No, no, not at all. I wouldn't go that far. I'm simply trying to look the facts unemotionally in the face. I'm trying to be realistic. I also contend that there is no real evil in what occurs naturally. I don't believe in seeing evil in everything. I leave that to the inquisitors.

BERENGER: And you consider all this natural?

DUDARD: What could be more natural than a rhinoceros?

BERENGER: Yes, but for a man to turn into a rhinoceros is abnormal beyond question.

DUDARD: Well, of course, that's a matter of opinion ...

BERENGER: It is beyond question, absolutely beyond question!

DUDARD: You seem very sure of yourself. Who can say where the normal stops and the abnormal begins? Can you personally define these conceptions of normality and abnormality? Nobody has solved this problem yet, either medically or philosophically. You ought to know that.

POINTS FOR DISCUSSION

1. Jean and Dudard typify two easily recognizable attitudes to new ideas—that of the radical revolutionary and that of the 'liberal'. What weaknesses in both these attitudes is Ionesco here satirizing?

2. What quality is it that Bérenger seems to possess which distinguishes him from Jean and Dudard?

3. What particular types of 'rhinoceritis' seem to you to be prevalent today?

4. MARGARET DRABBLE

THE MILLSTONE

MARGARET DRABBLE was born in 1939 and educated at Mount
School, York, and Newnham College, Cambridge. She has written
several very successful novels, a study of Wordsworth and a television
play, and is regarded as one of the most able and promising of the
younger writers in this country. Her novel *The Millstone* is about
Rosamund Stacey, an extremely intelligent young girl who has just
come down from the university with a degree in English. She lives
alone in her parents' flat in London, while they are abroad, and is
engaged on research for a doctorate. During this time she becomes
pregnant as a result of her first sexual experience and, rather to
the surprise of her sophisticated and intellectual friends, she decides
not to have an abortion. Alone, and with considerable courage, she
faces all the crises which her position involves her in, and when at last
the baby (whom she calls Octavia) is born, she is overwhelmed by love
for it. After a few months, however, she is told that Octavia has been
born with a serious condition of the lung which requires an immediate
and major operation. The first, short extract describes Rosamund's
feelings on the night before the operation.

When Rosamund goes to the hospital to visit Octavia after the
operation, she is refused admission by the nurses on the grounds that
visiting is not allowed in that particular ward. Rosamund persists fruit-
lessly in her demands to be let in and eventually, overcome by her
intense desire to see her child, she deliberately starts to scream very
loudly, and quickly falls into a fit of uncontrollable hysterics. It is this
that brings the surgeon on the scene and he immediately allows her to
visit Octavia as often as she wants to.

The novel as a whole is an account of the transition towards emotional
maturity of a girl who, for all her intellectual ability and apparent
sophistication, is basically afraid of life. There is nothing specifically
'religious' about it in the narrowest sense of that word. But it may help
towards a full discussion of the extracts to read (either beforehand or
afterwards) the following extract from a book on prayer by a Methodist
minister:[1]

> The fact remains that we do find ourselves in certain situations ask-
> ing for things God cannot give. There is a long tradition of asso-
> ciation between prayer and crisis; for example, when someone is

[1] J. Neville Ward: *The Use of Praying* (1968).

very ill and the doctors seem beaten, or in moments of danger when
our own or someone else's life is threatened, or on other occasions
of personal or national calamity or decision. Such experiences call
up from the depths of the mind the little frightened child everyone carries within, and when man becomes an infant crying in
the night he has no language but a cry. There is no point in
adopting a superior attitude to the self as under strain it regresses
to a level on which we hoped the mind would not again find itself
grovelling. This happens, and it must be accepted with charity
towards oneself. But we are functioning then as frightened humans
not as trusting Christians. As Christians we know that we must
be ready for all his perfect will; that is to say, we know that the
worst could happen and what matters is not what happens but
our doing God's will in it. Accordingly, spiritual growth invari-
ably implies movement away from fear of life towards a condition
of trusting God and wanting to serve him whichever way the cards
fall.

Both the following extracts should be read before attempting the
points for discussion.

(a) *The night before Octavia's operation*

The night before Octavia's operation I lay awake, enduring
what might have been my last battle with the vast shadowy
monsters of doubt. Some on such occasions must doubt the existence of God; it does not seem to me natural to survive such
disasters with faith unimpaired. I find it more honourable to take
events into consideration, when speaking of the mercy of God.
But, in fact, the subject of God did not much cross my mind, for I
had never given it much thought, having been brought up a
good Fabian rationalist, and notions such as the after-life and
heaven seem to me crude quite literally beyond belief. Justice,
however, preoccupied me. I could not rid myself of the notion
that if Octavia were to die, this would be a vengeance upon my
sin. The innocent shall suffer for the guilty. What my sin had been
I found difficult to determine, for I could not convince myself
that sleeping with George had been a sin; on the contrary, in
certain moods I tended to look on it as the only virtuous action
of my life. A sense of retribution nevertheless hung heavily over
me, and what I tried to preserve that night was faith not in God
but in the laws of chance.

Towards morning, I began to think that my sin lay in my love for her. For five minutes or so, I almost hoped that she might die, and thus relieve me of the corruption and the fatality of love. Ben Jonson said of his dead child, my sin was too much hope of thee, loved boy. We too easily take what the poets write as figures of speech, as pretty images, as strings of *bons mots*. Sometimes perhaps they speak the truth.

In the morning, when it was time to get up and get dressed and gather together her pitiably small requirements, I got out of bed and got down on my knees and said, Oh God, let her survive, let her live, let her be all right, and God was created by my need, perhaps.

(b) *Rosamund is admitted to the ward after succumbing to a violent fit of hysterics*

'Admit it, though,' I said. 'I only got in because I made a fuss. Other mothers don't get in, do they?'

'They don't all want to,' he said. 'They don't all have time to. Some of them have families at home to worry about. I wouldn't think about the others, if I were you. Think about yourself.'

So I did think about myself and I went on coming, regardless of all the others who couldn't come. They did not like me to be there, most of them, and they never found me a chair, but I wasn't bothered about a chair, and when I could not find one for myself I sat on the floor. It was quite peaceful, as she slept much of the time, so I was able to read and get bored in a fairly normal fashion. Sister Watkins would not speak to me, so deep was her resentment for what she had endured through my innocent agency, but the twinges of guilt that I felt whenever I encountered her were fainter than any I can recollect. Towards the end, however, try as I would, I could no longer stifle awareness of the other small ones, crying quietly and unheard behind their glass doors, or lying in a stupor of nothingness at the other end of the long ward, unprotected by partitions. There were only very small children in that part of the hospital; I did manage to see some larger ones, on one of my detours to the canteen, and some of them looked much better, and were reading and playing and shouting at each other. I saw some terrible sights, and even from time to time indulged the dreadful fancy that I was glad that Octavia's illness, however grave, had in no way marred her beauty. But this was but a fancy, for who would not rather endure a hare lip? Before Octavia was born, I used to think that love bore some relation to merit and to beauty, but now I saw that this was not so.

It must have been the saddest place in the world, that hospital. The décor made faint attempts at cheer, for there were friezes of bunny rabbits round the walls, and from time to time one particularly enthusiastic nurse would come and talk to me and dangle teddy bears at Octavia. Octavia took no interest in teddy bears, being at an age where she would play only with hard chewable objects or paper, but the nurse did not notice. I seemed to spend weeks there, for she was in for a long time, and during those weeks I saw only one other mother; we met, twice, at the entrance to the ward, and the second time accompanied each other more or less accidentally down to the canteen, where we sat, after brief and watery smiles, at the same table with our cups of tea. There seemed little small talk in which one could indulge, for any however trivial inquiry might well in those circumstances let loose unwelcome, dormant fear and tragedy, so finally all I said was, 'How did you manage to get in?' I wanted to talk to her, for she looked a nice woman: older than myself, with fair hair parted in the middle and draped looping gently backwards, and wearing a belted grey coat with a fur collar. Her face was one of those mild, round-chinned, long-cheeked faces, without angles or edges, but nevertheless shapely and memorable, with a kind of soft tranquility. She looked, too, as if she could talk, and I had had enough of my endless battle with the official and the inarticulate.

'Oh, I got in all right,' she said. 'I made them give it me in writing before I let him in, that I could come. Then all one has to do is show them the letter.'

'That shows foresight,' I said. 'I had to have hysterics.'

'Really?' she smiled, impressed. 'And it worked, did it?'

'Evidently.'

'I was always afraid,' she said, 'that if I made a real fuss, they wouldn't let me in anyway, because they'd say I was in too bad a state to see the children. I was afraid they'd put me to bed, too.'

I thought that this might well have been more than likely in my case too, and I thought about what Lydia had said about not being allowed to have an abortion because it would upset her;

degrees of madness were a tricky matter, it seemed, as were degrees of responsibility.

'Anyway,' I said, 'you didn't have to make a fuss. You did it all properly. I didn't realize what it would be like; if I'd realized I would have done something about it earlier too, perhaps.'

'One doesn't realize,' she said. 'The first time, I'd no idea. They wouldn't let me in with the first child. I had to get my husband to write a letter.'

'And that worked?'

'Oh yes. My husband has some influence here, you see. Some. I don't know what one would do without a little influence.' She smiled, wanly, and I noticed that she looked very, very tired.

'But how many children?' I asked. 'More than one child?'

'It's my second,' she said, 'that's in now. My second boy.'

There was a pause; she expected me to ask her what was wrong, perhaps, but I did not like to, and I could see that she was relieved by my abstention, for she went on, 'It's the same thing with both of them. So I knew it was coming this time, I've known for years. It makes it worse. People think it makes it better, but it makes it worse.'

'Why did you let him come here, after the other one?'

'Why? It's the best place, you know. They must have told you it's the best place.'

'Oh yes, they did. But I thought they said that everywhere.'

She smiled once more, her grave slow liquid smile, a smile not of amusement but of tired well-meaning. 'Oh no,' she said, 'it really is. You're very lucky. They really are wonderful here. It's your first, isn't it?'

'Yes, my first.'

'I wish you luck,' she said, finishing her cup of tea, 'with your second.'

'I'm not having any more,' I said.

'That's what I said,' she said. 'They said it wasn't likely to happen twice. And afterwards they told me the odds. Not that it matters. I'd have done it anyway.'

'But how,' I said, 'how do you bear it?' I did not mean to say it, but I said it in spite of myself and then wished I had not spoken, for her manner, though kind, had been impersonal, a sort of cool human sympathy rather than a personal interest. She did not mind, however; she seemed used to the question.

'I don't bear it,' she said. She picked up her spoon and started

to stir the leaves in the bottom of her cup, staring at them intently as though fate were indeed lying there amongst them, sod-
den and dark brown, to be altered by the movement of a tin
spoon. 'At first I used to pretend not to mind, I used to laugh it
off to my friends and underestimate its gravity when talking to
my family, you know what I mean. Extraordinary, the impulse
to play things down, don't you think? But in the end I got fed
up with it. I got tired of pretending it was nothing just to save
other people's feelings. Now I don't care who sees I care.'

She stopped talking as though she had said all she had to say.
I too said nothing, awed by this testimony of long-term sorrow.
There was still something in me that protested, that told me that
it was not possible that a mere accident of birth, the slight mis-
judgement of part of one organ should so mould and pin and
clamp a nature that it could grow like this, warped and graceful,
up the one sunny wall of dignity left to it. For, no doubt about it,
she wore her grief well: she spared herself and her associates the
additional infliction of ugliness, which so often accompanies much
pain.

We sat there for a moment or two, quietly, and I meant to say
no more, but after a while my nature returned, relentless, to its
preoccupations, like a dog to some old dried marrowless bone. I
could not help but ask; I had no hope of an answer, having always known that there is no answer, but it seemed to me that this
woman would at least understand the terms of my question.

'What,' I said to her then, 'what about all the others?'

'The others?' she said slowly.

'The others,' I said. 'Those that don't even get in. Those without money. Those without influence. Those who would not dare
to have hysterics.'

'Ah, those,' she said.

'Yes, those. What about them?'

'I don't know,' she said, still speaking slowly, her eyes still down-
cast. 'I don't know. I can't see that I can do anything about them.'

'But don't they worry you?' I said, reluctant to disturb her yet
unable to desist.

With difficulty she began to attach herself to the question. She
began to speak, and I waited with ridiculous expectation for her
answer.

'They used to worry me,' she said. 'When I first started on all
this, they worried me almost as much as my own. And I com-

forted myself by saying that nobody felt what I felt. They don't care, I said, or they would do what I do. But that's not true, of course.'

She looked at me for confirmation, and I nodded, for I agreed with what she had said.

'They do care,' she went on, 'but they don't set about it as I do. As time went on, though, and after years of this, I began to think that it was after all nothing to do with me. And it isn't, you know. My concerns are my concerns, and that's where it ends. I haven't the energy to go worrying about other people's children. They're nothing to do with me. I only have enough time to worry about myself. If I didn't put myself and mine first, they wouldn't survive. So I put them first and the others can look after themselves.'

She finished speaking; she had no more to say. I was, inevitably, touched almost to tears, for it is very rare that one meets someone who will give one such an answer to my question. She had spoken without harshness; I think it was that that had touched me most. I had so often heard these views expressed, but always before they had been accompanied by a guilty sneer at those who must be neglected, or a brisk Tory contempt for the ignorant, or a business-like blinkered air of proud realism. I had never heard them thus gently put forward as the result of sad necessity. I saw what she meant; I saw, in her, what all the others meant. I don't think I replied, and after a while she put on her gloves and stood up.

'Good-bye,' she said.

'Good-bye,' I said. And she went.

It was about a week later that I was able to take Octavia home. She was by this time quite gay and mobile once more, and seemingly unaffected, apart from loss of weight, by her ordeal. I arrived on the morning of her release with a small suitcase full of real clothes for her to wear; I had been looking forward to dressing her in something other than the white institutional nighties the hospital provided. In fact, I had whiled away some of my vigil by her cot-side by making her some new dresses; I had been taught at school to smock, an accomplishment I had never thought to use, but I do not like to let anything be wasted, and I had made her some very pretty small garments in various dark smart shades of Viyella. It had given me much satisfaction to make them; it was more profitable than jigsaws, for it actually saved money, while at the same time gratifying the need to do something mechanical with my hands, which otherwise occupied themselves by ripping holes in my cuticles or tearing strips off the wicker-seated chair I had finally acquired. I put her in my masterpiece to take her home: it was dark blue with a very small check. She looked very charming in it and jumped happily on my knee. I shook hands with all the nurses and even with Sister, who was glad to see me go. I got into the waiting taxi and off we went: I remembered the last time she and I had left the place together in this way, when she had been ten days old. I now knew better than to hope I would never have to go back again, for I knew that at the best she and I were in for a lifetime of checks and examinations, but nevertheless it seemed to me that I was more happy and more fortunate now than I had been then.

It was the middle of the afternoon: owing to the curious nature of the one-way street system, the quickest way to approach the flat was to go round Queens Crescent and then to the right off Portland Place. The air was bright and clear, and as we drove past the formal determined structure of the crescent, ever-demolished, ever-renewed, I suddenly thought that perhaps I could take it and survive. I had thought this before when drunk but never when sober; up till that moment I had been inwardly convinced that too much worry would rot my nature beyond any hope of fruit or even of flower. But then, however fleetingly, I felt that I could take what I had been given to take. I felt, for the first time since Octavia's birth, a sense of adequacy. Like Job, I had been threatened with the worst and, like Job, I had kept my shape. I knew something now of the quality of life, and anything in the way of happiness that I should hereafter receive would be based on fact and not on hope.

POINTS FOR DISCUSSION

1. Rosamund, on leaving the hospital, says she was 'more happy and more fortunate' than she had been when Octavia was first born. Why do you think this was so? Does the 'tone' of the passage give any idea of happiness in the conventional sense?

2. In the last sentence she refers to 'the quality of life'. What does she mean by this? What had she learnt?

3. Apart from the references to Job, is there any other evidence in the last paragraph that Rosamund's new view of life is influenced by religious ideas?

4. What do you think of the attitude towards suffering (both her own and that of other people) of the woman whom Rosamund met in the hospital? How does it differ from the attitudes to suffering expressed by some other writers in this book (e.g. Camus)? Is there anything in this passage to suggest that her attitude was not one of mere resignation? Do you admire her attitude?

5. Do you find the passage from the book on prayer (quoted in the introduction) in any way relevant to this extract?

5. ARTHUR KOESTLER

DARKNESS AT NOON

ARTHUR KOESTLER, now a naturalized British subject, was born in Budapest in 1905. He studied at Vienna University and was later political correspondent for a group of German newspapers and worked in the Middle East, Paris, Berlin, and Moscow. He was dismissed from this post because of his Communist allegiance, and travelled in Russia in 1932–3, but became disillusioned and finally broke with the Party in 1938. During the Spanish Civil War in 1936–7 he was correspondent for the *News Chronicle*; he was captured by Franco's troops and was kept in prison for ninety-six days under sentence of death before being eventually released.

Darkness at Noon, which is based on the actual experiences of some of Koestler's friends in Moscow, was first published in 1940 and is an account of the thoughts and experiences of an old Bolshevik, Nicolas Salmanovich Rubashov as he awaits his execution in a G.P.U. prison. Rubashov has been a devoted revolutionary for forty years; he has been a Commissar of the People and a leading member of the International, the aim of which is to foster revolutionary developments in other countries. But as those in control began to exercise dictatorial powers, Rubashov became disillusioned and eventually reached the conclusion that the State and the Party no longer represented the interests of the Revolution and the masses.

Rubashov is tortured by his own feelings of guilt; for, in the interests of preserving the Party, he had himself been responsible for the deaths of some of his former friends, including that of his secretary Arlova, who had developed political divergences. Recalling in his prison diary his convictions at that time he writes:

> Each wrong idea we follow is a crime committed against future generations. Therefore we have to punish wrong ideas as others punish crimes; with death. We were held for madmen because we followed every thought down to its final consequence and acted accordingly. We were compared to the inquisition because, like them, we constantly felt in ourselves the whole weight of responsibility for the superindividual life to come. We resembled the great Inquisitors in that we persecuted the seeds of evil not only in men's deeds but in their thoughts.

Now, however, he is assailed by doubt. 'I no longer believe in my infallibility. That is why I am lost.'

In the prison he is given his first hearing by Ivanov, an old college friend. Rubashov does not deny that he has deviated from the Party in that he has now 'placed the idea of man above the idea of mankind', but he resolutely denies the criminal charges brought against him, including one that he had conspired to assassinate 'No. 1.' Ivanov gives him a fortnight to decide whether to publish a confession or not.

In the first extract below it is the evening before this fortnight expires. The prisoners used to pass messages to each other by tapping out letters of the alphabet on the walls of their cells. By this means Rubashov has learnt that Bogrov, a former friend and a fellow-revolutionary, is about to be led out to execution. The last two extracts are from Rubashov's interview with Ivanov, which takes place just after Bogrov's execution.

The first two extracts should be read together; the third extract may be taken separately.

(a) *The execution of Bogrov*

Along the corridor came the low, hollow sound of subdued drumming. It was not tapping nor hammering: the men in the cells 380 to 402, who formed the acoustic chain and stood behind their doors like a guard of honour in the dark, brought out with deceptive resemblance the muffled, solemn sound of a roll of drums, carried by the wind from the distance. Rubashov stood with his eyes pressed to the spy-hole, and joined the chorus by beating with both hands rhythmically against the concrete door. To his astonishment, the stifled wave was carried on to the right, through No. 406 and beyond; Rip Van Winkle must have understood after all; he too was drumming. At the same time Rubashov heard to his left, at some distance still from the limits of his range of vision, the grinding of iron doors being rolled back on their slidings. The drumming to his left became slightly louder; Rubashov knew that the iron door which separated the isolation cells from the ordinary ones, had been opened. A bunch of keys jangled, now the iron door was shut again; now he heard the approach of steps, accompanied by sliding and slipping noises on the tiles. The drumming to the left rose in a wave, a steady, muffled crescendo. Rubashov's field of vision, limited by cells No. 401 and 470, was still empty. The sliding and squealing sounds approached quickly, now he distinguished also the moaning and whimpering, like the whimpering of a child. The steps quickened, the drumming to the left faded slightly, to the right it swelled.

Rubashov drummed. He gradually lost the sense of time and of space, he heard only the hollow beating as of jungle tomtoms; it might have been apes that stood behind the bars of their cages, beating their chests and drumming; he pressed his eye to the judas, rising and falling rhythmically on his toes as he drummed. As before, he saw only the stale, yellowish light of the electric bulb in the corridor; there was nothing to be seen save the iron doors of Nos. 401 and 470, but the roll of drums rose, and the creaking and whimpering approached. Suddenly shadowy figures entered his field of vision: they were there. Rubashov ceased to drum and stared. A second later they had passed.

What he had seen in these few seconds, remained branded on Rubashov's memory. Two dimly lit figures had walked past, both in uniform, big and indistinct, dragging between them a third, whom they held under the arms. The middle figure hung slack and yet with doll-like stiffness from their grasp, stretched out at length, face turned to the ground, belly arched downwards. The legs trailed after, the shoes skated along on the toes, producing the squealing sound which Rubashov had heard from the distance. Whitish strands of hair hung over the face turned towards the tiles, with the mouth wide open. Drops of sweat clung to it; out of the mouth spittle ran thinly down the chin. When they had dragged him out of Rubashov's field of vision, further to the right and down the corridor, the moaning and whimpering gradually faded away; it came to him only as a distant echo, consisting of three plaintive vowels: 'u-a-o'. But before they had turned the corner at the end of the corridor, by the barber's shop, Bogrov bellowed out loudly twice, and this time Rubashov heard not only the vowels, but the whole word; it was his own name, he heard it clearly: Ru-ba-shov.

Then, as if at a signal, silence fell. The electric lamps were burning as usual, the corridor was empty as usual. Only in the wall No. 406 was ticking:

ARISE, YE WRETCHED OF THE EARTH.

(b) *Ivanov describes the revolutionary's attitude to conscience*

'If I had a spark of pity for you,' he said, 'I would now leave you alone. But I have not a spark of pity. I drink; for a time, as you know, I drugged myself; but the vice of pity I have up till now managed to avoid. The smallest dose of it, and you are lost. Weeping over humanity and bewailing oneself—you know our race's pathological leaning to it. Our greatest poets destroyed themselves by this poison. Up to forty, fifty, they were revolutionaries —then they became consumed by pity and the world pronounced them holy. You appear to have the same ambition, and to believe it to be an individual process, personal to you, something unprecedented. . . .' He spoke rather louder and puffed out a cloud of smoke. 'Beware of these ecstasies,' he said. 'Every bottle of spirits contains a measurable amount of ecstasy. Unfortunately, only few people, particularly amongst our fellow countrymen, ever realize that the ecstasies of humility and suffering are as cheap as those induced chemically. The time when I woke from the anaesthetic, and found that my body stopped at the left knee, I also experienced a kind of absolute ecstasy of unhappiness. Do you remember the lectures you gave me at the time?' He poured out another glass and emptied it.

'My point is this,' he said; 'one may not regard the world as a sort of metaphysical brothel for emotions. That is the first commandment for us. Sympathy, conscience, disgust, despair, repentance, and atonement are for us repellent debauchery. To sit down and let oneself be hypnotized by one's own navel, to turn up one's eyes and humbly offer the back of one's neck to Gletkin's revolver—that is an easy solution. The greatest temptation for the like of us is: to renounce violence, to repent, to make peace with oneself. Most great revolutionaries fell before this temptation, from Spartacus to Danton and Dostoyevsky, they are the classical form of betrayal of the cause. The temptations of God were always more dangerous for mankind than those of Satan. As long as chaos dominates the world, God is an anachronism; and every compromise with one's own conscience is perfidy. When the accursed inner voice speaks to you, hold your hands over your ears. . . .'

He felt for the bottle behind him and poured out another glass.

Rubashov noticed that the bottle was already half empty. You also could do with a little solace, he thought.

'The greatest criminals in history,' Ivanov went on, 'are not of the type Nero and Fouché, but of the type Gandhi and Tolstoy. Gandhi's inner voice has done more to prevent the liberation of India than the British guns. To sell oneself for thirty pieces of silver is an honest transaction; but to sell oneself to one's own conscience is to abandon mankind. History is *a priori* amoral; it has no conscience. To want to conduct history according to the maxims of the Sunday school means to leave everything as it is. You know that as well as I do. You know the stakes in this game, and here you come talking about Bogrov's whimpering. . . .'

He emptied his glass and added:

'Or with conscience pricks because of your fat Arlova.'

POINTS FOR DISCUSSION

1. From the evidence in the second extract, would you say that Ivanov had a conscience? What is his attitude to conscience? How does this attitude differ from that held by the vast majority of western Europeans, whether Christian or not?

2. What do you learn about the psychology of revolutionaries both from Ivanov's remarks in the second extract and from Rubashov's prison diary quoted in the introduction?

3. In another part of the book, Rubashov says that 'the whimpering of Bogrov unbalanced the equation'. What do you think he means by this?

(c) *The problem of ends and means*

'I don't approve of mixing ideologies,' Ivanov continued. 'There are only two conceptions of human ethics, and they are at opposite poles. One of them is Christian and humane, declares the individual to be sacrosanct, and asserts that the rules of arithmetic are not to be applied to human units. The other starts from the basic principle that a collective aim justifies all means, and not only allows, but demands, that the individual should in every way be subordinated and sacrificed to the community—which may dispose of it as an experimentation rabbit or a sacrificial lamb. The first conception could be called anti-vivisection morality, the second, vivisection morality. Humbugs and dilettantes have always tried to mix the two conceptions; in practice, it is impossible. Whoever is burdened with power and responsibility finds out on the first occasion that he has to choose; and he is fatally driven to the second alternative. Do you know, since the establishment of Christianity as a state religion, a single example of a state which really followed a Christian policy? You can't point out one. In times of need—and politics are chronically in a time of need—the rulers were always able to evoke "exceptional circumstances", which demanded exceptional measures of defence. Since the existence of nations and classes, they live in a permanent state of mutual self-defence, which forces them eternally to defer to another time the putting into practice of humanism. . . .'

Rubashov looked through the window. The melted snow had again frozen and sparkled, an irregular surface of yellow-white crystals. The sentinel on the wall marched up and down with shouldered rifle. The sky was clear but moonless; above the machine-gun turret shimmered the Milky Way.

Rubashov shrugged his shoulders. 'Admit,' he said, 'that humanism and politics, respect for the individual and social progress, are incompatible. Admit, that Gandhi is a catastrophe for India; that chasteness in the choice of means leads to political impotence. In negatives we agree. But look where the other alternative has led us. . . .'

'Well,' asked Ivanov. 'Where?'

Rubashov rubbed his pince-nez on his sleeve, and looked at him shortsightedly. 'What a mess,' he said, 'what a mess we have made of our golden age.'

Ivanov smiled. 'Maybe,' he said happily. 'Look at the Gracchi and Saint-Just and the Commune of Paris. Up to now, all revolutions have been made by moralizing dilettantes. They were always in good faith and perished because of their dilettantism. We for the first time are consequent. . . .'

'Yes,' said Rubashov. 'So consequent, that in the interests of a just distribution of land we deliberately let die of starvation about five million farmers and their families in one year. So consequent were we in the liberation of human beings from the shackles of industrial liberation that we sent about ten million people to do forced labour in the Arctic regions and the jungles of the East, under conditions similar to those of antique galley slaves. So consequent that, to settle a difference of opinion, we know only one argument: death, whether it is a matter of submarines, manure, or the Party line to be followed in Indo-China. Our engineers work with the constant knowledge that an error in calculation may take them to prison or the scaffold; the higher officials in our administration ruin and destroy their subordinates, because they know that they will be held responsible for the slightest slip and be destroyed themselves; our poets settle discussions on questions of style by denunciation to the Secret Police, because the expressionists consider the naturalistic style counter-revolutionary, and vice versa. Acting consequentially in the interests of the coming generations, we have laid such terrible privations on the present one that its average length of life is shortened by a quarter. In order to defend the existence of the country, we have had to take exceptional measures and make transition-stage laws, which are in every point contrary to the aims of the Revolution. The people's standard of life is lower than it was before the Revolution; the labour conditions are harder, the discipline is more inhuman, the piece-work drudgery worse than in colonial countries with native coolies; we have lowered the age limit for capital punishment down to twelve years; our sexual laws are more narrow-minded than those of England, our leader-worship more Byzantine than that of the reactionary dictatorships. Our Press and our schools cultivate Chauvinism, militarism, dogmatism, conformism, and ignorance. The arbitrary power of the Government is unlimited, and unexampled in history; freedom of the Press, of opinion and of movement are as thoroughly exterminated as though the proclamation of the Rights of Man had never been. We have built up the most gigantic police apparatus, with informers made a national institution, and with the most refined scientific system of physical and mental torture. We whip the groaning masses of the country towards a theoretical future happiness, which only we can see. For the energies of this generation are exhausted; they were spent in the Revolution; for this generation is bled white and there is nothing left of it but a moaning, numbed, apathetic lump of sacrificial flesh.... Those are the consequences of our consequentialness. You called it vivisection morality. To me it sometimes seems as though the experimenters had torn the skin off the victim and left it standing with bared tissues, muscles and nerves....'

'Well, and what of it?' said Ivanov happily. 'Don't you find it wonderful? Has anything more wonderful ever happened in history? We are tearing the old skin off mankind and giving it a new one. That is not an occupation for people with weak nerves; but there was once a time when it filled you with enthusiasm. What has changed you that you are now as pernickety as an old maid?'

Rubashov wanted to answer: 'Since then I have heard Bogrov call out my name.' But he knew that this answer did not make sense. So he answered instead:

'To continue with the same metaphor: I see the flayed body of this generation: but I see no trace of the new skin. We all thought one could treat history like one experiments in physics. The difference is that in physics one can repeat the experiment a thousand times, but in history only once. Danton and Saint-Just can be sent to the scaffold only once; and if it should turn out that big submarines would after all have been the right thing, Comrade Bogrov will not come to life again.'

'And what follows?' asked Ivanov. 'Should we sit with idle hands because the consequences of an act are never quite to be foreseen, and hence all action is evil? We vouch for every act with our heads—more cannot be expected of us. In the opposite camp they are not so scrupulous. Any old idiot of a general can experiment with thousands of living bodies; and if he makes a mistake, he will at most be retired. The forces of reaction and counter-revolution have no scruples or ethical problems. Imagine a Sulla, a Galliffet, a Kolchak reading Raskolnikov. Such peculiar birds as you are found only in the trees of revolution. For the others it is easier....'

He looked at his watch. The cell window had turned a dirty grey; the newspaper which was stuck over the broken pane swelled and rustled in the morning breeze. On the rampart opposite, the sentry was still doing his hundred steps up and down.

'For a man with your past,' Ivanov went on, 'this sudden revulsion against experimenting is rather naïve. Every year several million people are killed quite pointlessly by epidemics and other natural catastrophes. And we should shrink from sacrificing a few hundred thousand for the most promising experiment in history? Not to mention the legions of those who die of undernourishment and tuberculosis in coal and quicksilver mines, rice-fields and cotton plantations. No one takes any notice of them; nobody asks why or what for; but if here we shoot a few thousand objectively harmful people, the humanitarians all over the world foam at the mouth. Yes, we liquidated the parasitic part of the peasantry and let it die of starvation. It was a surgical operation which had to be done once and for all; but in the good old days before the Revolution just as many died in any dry year—only senselessly and pointlessly. The victims of the Yellow River floods in China amount sometimes to hundreds of thousands. Nature is generous in her senseless experiments on mankind. Why should mankind not have the right to experiment on itself?'

He paused; Rubashov did not answer. He went on:

'Have you ever read brochures of an anti-vivisectionist society? They are shattering and heartbreaking; when one reads how some poor cur which has had its liver cut out, whines and licks his tormentor's hands, one is just as nauseated as you were tonight. But if these people had their say, we would have no serums against cholera, typhoid, or diphtheria. . . .'

He emptied the rest of the bottle, yawned, stretched and stood up. He limped over to Rubashov at the window, and looked out.

'It's getting light,' he said. 'Don't be a fool, Rubashov. Everything I brought up tonight is elementary knowledge, which you know as well as I. You were in a state of nervous depression, but now it is over.' He stood next to Rubashov at the window, with his arm round Rubashov's shoulders; his voice was nearly tender. 'Now go and sleep it off, old warhorse; tomorrow the time is up, and we will both need a clear head to concoct your deposition. Don't shrug your shoulders—you are yourself at least half convinced that you will sign. If you deny it, it's just moral cowardice. Moral cowardice has driven many to martyrdom.'

Rubashov looked out into the grey light. The sentry was just doing a right-about turn. Above the machine-gun turret the sky was pale grey, with a shade of red. 'I'll think it over again,' said Rubashov after a while.

When the door had closed behind his visitor, Rubashov knew that he had already half-surrendered. He threw himself on the bunk, exhausted and yet strangely relieved. He felt hollowed-out and sucked dry, and at the same time as if a weight had been lifted from him. Bogrov's pathetic appeal had in his memory lost some

of its acoustic sharpness. Who could call it betrayal if, instead of
the dead, one held faith with the living?

POINTS FOR DISCUSSION

1. 'The principle that the end justifies the means is and remains the
only rule of political ethics; anything else is just vague chatter and
melts away between one's fingers.' This remark is made by Ivanov in
another part of the interview; consider the truth of this.

2. 'Nature is generous in her senseless experiments on mankind. Why
should mankind not have the right to experiment on itself?' What do
you think of this line of thought?

3. Summarize the essential differences between the points of view of
Ivanov and Rubashov.

4. Koestler heads this chapter with the following quotation from a
fifteenth-century bishop:

> 'When the existence of the Church is threatened, she is released
> from the commandments of morality.... For all order is for the
> sake of the community and the individual must be sacrificed to the
> common good.'

Why do you think Koestler does this?

6. GRAHAM GREENE

THE POWER AND THE GLORY

GRAHAM GREENE has been one of the most prominent English writers since the 1930s. He was born in 1904 and became a Roman Catholic in 1926. Many of his novels and plays are concerned with specifically religious themes, such as the conflict between good and evil, the question of damnation or salvation, or the long struggles of man in his search for God in an apparently hostile world. In dealing with these themes, it is characteristic of Greene to take as his leading characters those whom the world would class as failures or outcasts, whether it is the boy gangster, Pinkie, in *Brighton Rock*, the unsuccessful police officer in *The Heart of the Matter* or the 'whisky priest' in *The Power and the Glory*. He shows a marked preoccupation with the weak, the criminal, and the unsuccessful, and indeed the whole 'seediness' of the world which such people inhabit. Fear, violence, cruelty, loneliness, and frustration all play a large part in his writings. Some may find tiresome this persistent interest in the drabness and squalor of life, but for Greene this 'seediness' had a very deep appeal ('It seems to represent a stage further back') and it is in these surroundings of ugliness and despair, and very often of violence, that he works out the problems of the 'appalling strangeness of the mercy of God' to which his faith commits him.

In 1938 Greene visited Mexico in order to write a study of religious persecution under the communist regime. He published an account of his travels in *The Lawless Roads,* from which this quotation may help to explain the fascination which such grim and violent surroundings held for him:

> In the plaza the same insolent stares and veiled gibes. I went back to the patio and read the women's magazines. There was an advertisement for a Reference Library for Sub-Debs. 'A date to remember. How to put yourself across so boys will never forget you.' Three cents. 'Tables for Ladies. How do you rate with boys? Here's a talent test for you.' Three cents. 'Rating for dating. The famous sub-deb chart for getting along with boys.' Three cents.
>
> I loathed Mexico—but there were times when it seemed as if there were worse places. . . . Here were idolatry and oppression, starvation and casual violence, but you lived under the shadow of religion—of God or the Devil. 'Rating for Dating'—it wasn't evil, it wasn't

anything at all, it was just the drugstore and the Coca-Cola, the hamburger, the sinless empty graceless chromium world.

In *The Lawless Roads* are mentioned many of the people whom Greene was later to develop as characters in *The Power and the Glory*. The novel is set at a time of intense religious persecution, when all the priests have either fled, or have been shot or have submitted to the regime by marrying. One priest remains and is being pursued by police officials as he travels from place to place trying to celebrate Mass and to hear confessions as often as he can. The priest is a wreck and a failure by worldly standards; apart from being a drunkard, he has had an illegitimate daughter by a peasant woman. Towards the end of the book, when a means of escape over the border is offered to him, he is suddenly called to give the last sacrament to a dying American gangster; although he is well aware that this is a trap to catch him, he goes and is captured by the police and eventually shot. An important character in the book is the police lieutenant. Greene says of him : 'I had to invent him as a counter to the failed priest; the idealistic police officer who stifled life from the best possible motives; the drunken priest who continued to pass life on.'

In the first extract, the priest, who has been arrested on the previous day, is being taken by the lieutenant to prison; in the second extract the priest is alone in his prison cell on the night before his execution.

(a) *The priest's view of the love of God*

'You're a man of education,' the lieutenant said. He lay across the entrance of the hut with his head on the rolled cape and his revolver by his side. It was night, but neither man could sleep. The priest, when he shifted, groaned a little with stiffness and cramp; the lieutenant was in a hurry to get home, and they had ridden till midnight. They were down off the hills and in the marshy plain. Soon the whole State would be subdivided by swamp. The rains had really begun.

'I'm not that. My father was a storekeeper.'

'I mean, you've been abroad. You can talk like a Yankee. You've had schooling.'

'Yes.'

'I've had to think things out for myself. But there are some things which you don't have to learn in a school. That there are rich and poor.' He said in a low voice: 'I've shot three hostages because of you. Poor men. It made me hate you.'

'Yes,' the priest admitted, and tried to stand to ease the cramp in his right thigh. The lieutenant sat quickly up, gun in hand: 'What are you doing?'

'Nothing. Just cramp. That's all.' He lay down again with a groan.

The lieutenant said: 'Those men I shot. They were my own people. I wanted to give them the whole world.'

'Well, who knows? Perhaps that's what you did.'

The lieutenant spat suddenly, viciously, as if something un-clean had got upon his tongue. He said: 'You always have answers which mean nothing.'

'I was never any good at books,' the priest said. 'I haven't any memory. But there was one thing always puzzled me about men like yourself. You hate the rich and love the poor. Isn't that right?'

'Yes.'

'Well, if I hated you, I wouldn't want to bring my child to be like you. It's not sense.'

'That's just twisting . . .'

'Perhaps it is. I've never got your ideas straight. We've always said the poor are blessed and the rich are going to find it hard to get into heaven. Why should we make it hard for the poor man too? Oh, I know we are told to give to the poor, to see they are not hungry—hunger can make a man do evil just as much as money can. But why should we give the poor power? It's better to let him die in dirt and wake in heaven—so long as we don't push his face in the dirt.'

'I hate your reasons,' the lieutenant said. 'I don't want reasons. If you see somebody in pain, people like you reason and reason. You say—perhaps pain's a good thing, perhaps he'll be better for it one day. I want to let my heart speak.'

'At the end of a gun.'

'Yes. At the end of a gun.'

'Oh well, perhaps when you're my age you'll know the heart's an untrustworthy beast. The mind is too, but it doesn't talk about love. Love. And a girl puts her head under water or a child's strangled, and the heart all the time says love, love.'

They lay quiet for a while in the hut. The priest thought the lieutenant was asleep until he spoke again. 'You never talk straight. You say one thing to me—but to another man, or a woman, you say: "God is love." But you think that stuff won't go down with me, so you say different things. Things you think I'll agree with.'

'Oh,' the priest said, 'that's another thing altogether—God *is* love. I don't say the heart doesn't feel a taste of it, but what a taste. The smallest glass of love mixed with a pint pot of ditch-water. We wouldn't recognize *that* love. It might even look like hate. It would be enough to scare us—God's love. It set fire to a bush in the desert, didn't it, and smashed open graves and set the dead walking in the dark. Oh, a man like me would run a mile to get away if he felt that love around.'

'You don't trust him much, do you? He doesn't seem a grateful kind of God. If a man served me well as you've served him, well, I'd recommend him for promotion, see he got a good pension ... if he was in pain, with cancer, I'd put a bullet through his head.'

'Listen,' the priest said earnestly, leaning forward in the dark, pressing on a cramped foot, 'I'm not as dishonest as you think I am. Why do you think I tell people out of the pulpit that they're in danger of damnation if death catches them unawares? I'm not telling them fairy stories I don't believe myself. I don't know a thing about the mercy of God: I don't know how awful the human heart looks to Him. But I do know this—that if there's ever been a single man in this state damned, then I'll be damned too.' He said slowly: 'I wouldn't want it to be any different. I just want justice, that's all.'

POINTS FOR DISCUSSION

1. What seem to be the aspects of the Church and its teaching which the lieutenant hates? How far do you sympathize with his feelings?

2. What do you think of the priests's remarks about the love of God?

3. Do you agree with the lieutenant in his remark to the priest, 'He doesn't seem a grateful kind of God.'?

(b) Saint or sinner?

The priest sat on the floor, holding the brandy-flask. Presently he unscrewed the cap and put his mouth to it. The spirit didn't do a thing to him: it might have been water. He put it down again and began some kind of a general confession, speaking in a whisper. He said: 'I have committed fornication.' The formal phrase meant nothing at all: it was like a sentence in a newspaper: you couldn't feel repentance over a thing like that. He started again: 'I have lain with a woman,' and tried to imagine the other priest asking him: 'How many times? Was she married?' 'No.' Without thinking what he was doing, he took another drink of brandy.

As the liquid touched his tongue he remembered his child, coming in out of the glare: the sullen unhappy knowledgeable face. He said: 'Oh God, help her. Damn me, I deserve it, but let her live for ever.' This was the love he should have felt for every soul in the world: all the fear and the wish to save concentrated unjustly on the one child. He began to weep; it was as if he had to watch her from the shore drown slowly because he had forgotten how to swim. He thought: This is what I should feel all the time for everyone, and he tried to turn his brain away towards the half-caste, the lieutenant, even a dentist he had once sat with for a few minutes, the child at the banana station, calling up a long succession of faces, pushing at his attention as if it were a heavy door which wouldn't budge. For those were all in danger too. He prayed: 'God help them,' but in the moment of prayer he switched back to his child beside the rubbish-dump, and he knew it was for her only that he prayed. Another failure.

After a while he began again: 'I have been drunk—I don't know how many times; there isn't a duty I haven't neglected; I have been guilty of pride, lack of charity....' The words were becoming formal again, meaning nothing. He had no confessor to turn his mind away from the formula to the fact.

He took another drink of brandy, and getting up with pain because of his cramp, he moved to the door and looked through the bars at the hot moony square. He could see the police asleep in their hammocks, and one man who couldn't sleep lazily rocking up and down, up and down. There was an odd silence everywhere, even in the other cells; it was as if the whole world had tactfully turned away to avoid seeing him die. He felt his way back along the wall to the farthest corner and sat down with the flask between his knees. He thought: If I hadn't been so useless, useless. . . . The eight hard hopeless years seemed to him to be only a caricature of service: a few communions, a few confessions, and an endless bad example. He thought: If I had only one soul to offer, so that I could say, Look what I've done. . . . People had died for him, they had deserved a saint, and a tinge of bitterness spread across his mind for their sake that God hadn't thought fit to send them one. Padre José and me, and he took a drink again from the brandy flask. He thought of the cold faces of the saints rejecting him.

The night was slower than the last he had spent in prison because he was alone. Only the brandy, which he finished about two in the morning, gave him any sleep at all. He felt sick with fear, his stomach ached, and his mouth was dry with the drink. He began to talk aloud to himself because he couldn't stand the silence any more. He complained miserably: 'It's all very well . . . for saints,' and later: 'How does he know it only lasts a second? How long's a second?'; then he began to cry, beating his head gently against the wall. They had given a chance to Padre José, but they had never given him a chance at all. Perhaps they had got it all wrong—just because he had escaped them for such a time. Perhaps they really thought he would refuse the conditions Padre José had accepted, that he would refuse to marry, that he was proud. Perhaps if he suggested it himself, he would escape yet. The hope calmed him for a while, and he fell asleep with his head against the wall. . . . When he woke up it was dawn. He woke with a huge feeling of hope which suddenly and completely left him at the first sight of the prison yard. It was the morning of his death. He crouched on the floor with the empty brandy-flask in his hand trying to remember an Act of Contrition. 'O God, I am sorry and beg pardon for all my sins . . . crucified . . . worthy of thy dreadful punishments.' He was confused, his mind was on other things: it was not the good death for which one always prayed. He caught sight of his own shadow on the cell wall; it had a look of surprise and grotesque unimportance. What a fool he had been to think that he was strong enough to stay when others fled. What an impossible fellow I am, he thought, and how useless. I have done nothing for anybody. I might just as well have never lived. His parents were dead—soon he wouldn't even be a memory—perhaps after all he wasn't really Hellworthy. Tears poured down his face; he was not at the moment afraid of damnation—even the fear of pain was in the background. He felt only an immense disappointment because he had to go to God empty-handed, with nothing done at all. It seemed to him, at that moment, that it would have been quite easy to have been a saint. It would only have needed a little self-restraint and a little courage. He felt like someone who has missed happiness by seconds at an appointed place. He knew now that at the end there was only one thing that counted—to be a saint.

POINTS FOR DISCUSSION

1. What is the conventional idea of a saint?
2. What qualities of a saint does Greene intend us to see in the priest?
3. 'There is something repellent about a faith that can produce such self-reproach and despair.' Do you agree with this comment?
4. Re-read the quotation from *The Lawless Roads* in the introduction to this extract. How would you counter this attitude of Greene as it is reflected in this extract?

7. SAMUEL BECKETT

WAITING FOR GODOT

SAMUEL BECKETT was born near Dublin in 1906. After taking his B.A. at Trinity College, where he read French and Italian, he was selected for the post of an exchange lecturer at the Ecole Normale Superieure in Paris. While in Paris he met and formed a close association with James Joyce. He returned to Trinity College with a lectureship in 1931 but gave it up after a few months. There followed some years of a rather unsettled existence in France, Germany, and elsewhere in Europe but he finally settled in Paris in 1937. Although in Ireland at the outbreak of war in 1939, he returned to Paris and eventually joined a resistance group, which involved him in a period of hiding from the Gestapo in the Vaucluse, near Avignon, where he worked as an agricultural labourer.

Beckett, who writes mainly in French, has published several poems, plays, short stories, and novels. *Waiting for Godot* is his best known play and was first produced in Paris in 1953 and in London in 1955. He was awarded a Nobel Prize for Literature in 1969.

The plays of Beckett, together with those of other writers such as Ionesco and Pinter, have frequently been classified under the label 'Absurd Drama' or 'The Theatre of the Absurd', although these writers do not consciously regard themselves as forming part of a school or movement. But they have this much in common, that they have dispensed with most of the standards by which drama has been judged in the past; all that we have come to expect of a good play in terms of construction, logical development, characterization, and intelligent dialogue has disappeared; instead the development (such as it is) seems arbitrary and not logical, the plot non-existent or bewilderingly inconsequential and the dialogue banal or incoherent. In addition, the settings and characters are often highly bizarre; in Beckett's *Endgame*, for example, the leading character, Hamm, is disabled and unable to walk, while his servant, Clov, is unable to sit down; Hamm's legless parents, Nagg and Nell, are shut up in two dustbins which stand on the stage. Or in his *Happy Days*, Winnie symbolizes the human predicament by appearing buried up to her waist in a mound of earth, and slowly sinking; her husband Willie meanwhile remains absorbed in his newspaper.

It is hardly surprising that such plays have often been dismissed as meaningless or outrageous, or that they have met with bewilderment and even abuse. Nevertheless, they are now an accepted part of the theatrical scene. *Waiting for Godot* is a highly successful play by any standards, and has been translated into about twenty languages. The appeal of such plays is strong because they take as their starting-point *not* a world united and held together by a common and firmly main-tained belief about man and his purpose in life, but rather a world which, after two world wars and the horrors that ensued, has for many people lost its sense and meaning. From this 'absurd'[1] world, religious certainties have vanished, and substitutes for religion have been found arid and ineffective; individuality seems in danger of being engulfed in the mechanical conformity of society, and language itself seems to be losing its power to communicate; an air of disillusionment and spiritual *malaise* prevails. It would be a gross exaggeration to say that this is the characteristic spirit of our times; nevertheless, most people today have experienced this feeling of disintegration and disillusionment—hence the appeal to so many people of the Theatre of the Absurd. Like the dramatists of fifth-century Athens, Beckett and his contemporaries seem to be genuinely and ruthlessly grappling with the insoluble prob-lems of life and to be directing audiences to thinking about the purpose of man in the universe. In his book *The Theatre of the Absurd*, Martin Esslin has this comment to make:

> In expressing the tragic sense of loss at the disappearance of ulti-mate certainties the Theatre of the Absurd, by a strange paradox, is also a symptom of what probably comes nearest to being a genuine religious quest in our age; an effort, however timid and tentative, to sing, to laugh, to weep—and to growl—if not in praise of God... at least in search of a dimension of the In-effable... For God is dead, above all, to the masses who live from day to day and have lost all contact with the basic facts—and mysteries—of the human condition with which, in former times, they were kept in touch through the living ritual of their religion, which made them parts of a real community and not just atoms in an atomised society.

The setting of *Waiting for Godot* is a country road on which two tramps, Vladimir and Estragon, are waiting for an appointment with a Mr. Godot. At the end of Act 1 they learn from a boy, Mr. Godot's messenger, that he cannot come but that he will definitely come on the next day. In Act II precisely the same thing happens; they wait, and the boy arrives with the same message—that Mr. Godot will come tomorrow, not today.

The first extract comes from very early on in the play, which is full of silences and unfinished conversations; Vladimir has just commented, apropos of nothing in particular. 'One of the thieves was saved ...

---

[1] For an explanation of this use of the word 'absurd' see the introduction to the extract from *The Plague* by Albert Camus on page 1.

It's a reasonable percentage.' A few lines later on he takes up the same point again.

The second extract comes from Act II and recounts the second visit of the boy. He is apparently the same boy who has appeared the day before, although he denies this.

Both the extracts should be read before attempting the points for discussion.

(a) *'One of the thieves was saved. . . . It's a reasonable percentage.'*

VLADIMIR: ... Gogo.

ESTRAGON [*irritably*]: What is it?

VLADIMIR: Did you ever read the Bible?

ESTRAGON: The Bible ... [*He reflects.*] I must have taken a look at it.

VLADIMIR: Do you remember the Gospels?

ESTRAGON: I remember the maps of the Holy Land. Coloured they were. Very pretty. The Dead Sea was pale blue. The very look of it made me thirsty. That's where we'll go, I used to say, that's where we'll go for our honeymoon. We'll swim. We'll be happy.

VLADIMIR: You should have been a poet.

ESTRAGON: I was [*Gestures towards his rags.*] Isn't that obvious?

Silence.

VLADIMIR: Where was I ... How's your foot?

ESTRAGON: Swelling visibly.

VLADIMIR: Ah yes, the two thieves. Do you remember the story?

ESTRAGON: No.

VLADIMIR: Shall I tell it to you?

ESTRAGON: No.

VLADIMIR: It'll pass the time. [*Pause.*] Two thieves, crucified at the same time as our Saviour. One——

ESTRAGON: Our what?

VLADIMIR: Our Saviour. Two thieves. One is supposed to have been saved and the other ... [*he searches for the contrary of saved*] ... damned.

ESTRAGON: Saved from what?

VLADIMIR: Hell.

ESTRAGON: I'm going.

He does not move.

VLADIMIR: And yet ... [*pause*] ... how is it—this is not boring you I hope—how is it that of the four Evangelists only one speaks of a thief being saved. The four of them were there— or thereabouts—and only one speaks of a thief being saved. [*Pause.*] Come on, Gogo, return the ball, can't you, once in a way?

ESTRAGON [*with exaggerated enthusiasm*]: I find this really most extraordinarily interesting.

VLADIMIR: One out of four. Of the other three two don't mention any thieves at all and the third says that both of them abused him.

ESTRAGON: Who?

VLADIMIR: What?

ESTRAGON: What's all this about? Abused who?

VLADIMIR: The Saviour.

ESTRAGON: Why?

VLADIMIR: Because he wouldn't save them.

ESTRAGON: From hell?

VLADIMIR: Imbecile! From death.

ESTRAGON: I thought you said hell.

VLADIMIR: From death, from death.

ESTRAGON: Well, what of it?

VLADIMIR: Then the two of them must have been damned.

ESTRAGON: And why not?

VLADIMIR: But one of the four says that one of the two was saved.

ESTRAGON: Well? They don't agree, and that's all there is to it.

VLADIMIR: But all four were there. And only one speaks of a thief being saved. Why believe him rather than the others?

ESTRAGON: Who believes him?

VLADIMIR: Everybody. It's the only version they know.

ESTRAGON: People are bloody ignorant apes.

He rises painfully, goes limping to extreme left, halts, gazes into distance off with his hand screening his eyes, turns, goes to extreme right, gazes into distance. Vladimir watches him, then goes and picks up the boot, peers into it, drops it hastily.

VLADIMIR: Pah!

He spits. Estragon moves to centre, halts with his back to the auditorium.

ESTRAGON: Charming spot. [*He turns, advances to front, halts facing auditorium.*] Inspiring prospects. [*He turns to Vladimir*]. Let's go.

VLADIMIR: We can't.

ESTRAGON: Why not?

VLADIMIR: We're waiting for Godot.

ESTRAGON: [*despairingly*]. Ah! [*Pause.*] You're sure it was here?

VLADIMIR: What?

ESTRAGON: That we were to wait.

VLADIMIR: He said by the tree. [*They look at the tree.*] Do you see any others?

ESTRAGON: What is it?

VLADIMIR: I don't know. A willow.

ESTRAGON: Where are the leaves?

VLADIMIR: It must be dead.

ESTRAGON: No more weeping.

VLADIMIR: Or perhaps it's not the season.

ESTRAGON: Looks to me more like a bush.

VLADIMIR: A shrub.

ESTRAGON: A bush.

VLADIMIR: A——. What are you insinuating? That we've come to the wrong place?

ESTRAGON: He should be here.

VLADIMIR: He didn't say for sure he'd come.

ESTRAGON: And if he doesn't come?

VLADIMIR: We'll come back tomorrow.

ESTRAGON: And then the day after tomorrow.

VLADIMIR: Possibly.

ESTRAGON: And so on.

VLADIMIR: The point is—

ESTRAGON: Until he comes.

VLADIMIR: You're merciless.

ESTRAGON: We came here yesterday.

VLADIMIR: Ah no, there you're mistaken.

ESTRAGON: What did we do yesterday?

VLADIMIR: What did we do yesterday?

ESTRAGON: Yes.

VLADIMIR: Why ... [*Angrily.*] Nothing is certain when you're about.

ESTRAGON: In my opinion we were here.

VLADIMIR [*looking round*]: You recognize the place?

ESTRAGON: I didn't say that.

VLADIMIR: Well?

ESTRAGON: That makes no difference.

VLADIMIR: All the same ... that tree ... [*turning towards the auditorium*] ... that bog.

ESTRAGON: You're sure it was this evening?

VLADIMIR: What?

ESTRAGON: That we were to wait.

VLADIMIR: He said Saturday. [*Pause.*] I think.

ESTRAGON: You think.

VLADIMIR: I must have made a note of it.

    He fumbles in his pockets, bursting with miscellaneous rubbish.

ESTRAGON [*very insidious*]: But what Saturday? And is it Saturday? Is it not rather Sunday? [*Pause.*] Or Monday? [*Pause.*] Or Friday?

VLADIMIR [*looking wildly about him, as though the date was inscribed in the landscape*]: It's not possible!

ESTRAGON: Or Thursday?

VLADIMIR: What'll we do?

ESTRAGON: If he came yesterday and we weren't here you may be sure he won't come here again today.

VLADIMIR: But you say we were here yesterday.

ESTRAGON: I may be mistaken. [*Pause.*] Let's stop talking for a minute, do you mind?

(b) *A message from Mr. Godot*

BOY: Mister ... [*Vladimir turns.*] Mr. Albert ...

VLADIMIR: Off we go again. [*Pause.*] Do you not recognize me?

BOY: No, sir.

VLADIMIR: It wasn't you came yesterday.

BOY: No, sir.

VLADIMIR: This is your first time.

BOY: Yes, sir.

    Silence.

VLADIMIR: You have a message from Mr. Godot.

BOY: Yes, sir.

VLADIMIR: He won't come this evening.

BOY: No, sir.

VLADIMIR: But he'll come tomorrow.

BOY: Yes, sir.

VLADIMIR: Without fail.

BOY: Yes, sir.

  Silence.

VLADIMIR: Did you meet anyone?

BOY: No, sir.

VLADIMIR: Two other ... [*he hesitates*] ... men?

BOY: I didn't see anyone, sir.

  Silence.

VLADIMIR: What does he do, Mr. Godot? [*Silence.*] Do you hear
  me?

BOY: Yes, sir.

VLADIMIR: Well?

BOY: He does nothing, sir.

  Silence.

VLADIMIR: How is your brother?

BOY: He's sick, sir.

VLADIMIR: Perhaps it was he came yesterday.

BOY: I don't know, sir.

  Silence.

VLADIMIR [*softly*]: Has he a beard, Mr. Godot?

BOY: Yes, sir.

VLADIMIR: Fair or ... [*he hesitates*] ... or black?

BOY: I think it's white, sir.

  Silence.

VLADIMIR: Christ have mercy on us!

  Silence.

BOY: What am I to tell Mr. Godot, sir.

VLADIMIR: Tell him ... [*he hesitates*] ... tell him you saw me and
  that ... [*he hesitates*] ... that you saw me. [*Pause. Vladimir
  advances, the Boy recoils. Vladimir halts, the Boy halts. With
  sudden violence*] You're sure you saw me, you won't come and
  tell me tomorrow that you never saw me! [*Silence. Vladimir
  makes a sudden spring forward, the Boy avoids him and exits
  running. Silence. The sun sets, the moon rises. As in Act I.
  Vladimir stands motionless and bowed. Estragon wakes, takes
  off his boots, gets up with one in each hand and goes and puts
  them down centre front, then goes towards Vladimir.*]

ESTRAGON: What's wrong with you?

VLADIMIR: Nothing.

ESTRAGON: I'm going.

VLADIMIR: So am I.

ESTRAGON: Was I long asleep?

VLADIMIR: I don't know.

   Silence.

ESTRAGON: Where shall we go?

VLADIMIR: Not far.

ESTRAGON: Oh, yes, let's go far away from here.

VLADIMIR: We can't.

ESTRAGON: Why not?

VLADIMIR: We have to come back tomorrow.

ESTRAGON: What for?

VLADIMIR: To wait for Godot.

ESTRAGON: Ah! [*Silence.*] He didn't come?

VLADIMIR: No.

ESTRAGON: And now it's too late.

VLADIMIR: Yes, now it's night.

ESTRAGON: And if we dropped him? [*Pause.*] If we dropped him?

VLADIMIR: He'd punish us. [*Silence. He looks at the tree.*] Everything's dead but the tree.

ESTRAGON [*looking at the tree*]: What is it?

VLADIMIR: It's the tree.

ESTRAGON: Yes, but what kind?

VLADIMIR: I don't know. A willow.

   [*Estragon draws Vladimir towards the tree. They stand
   motionless before it. Silence.*]

ESTRAGON: Why don't we hang ourselves?

VLADIMIR: With what?

ESTRAGON: You haven't got a bit of rope?

VLADIMIR: No.

ESTRAGON: Then we can't.

   Silence.

VLADIMIR: Let's go.

ESTRAGON: Wait, there's my belt.

VLADIMIR: It's too short.

ESTRAGON: You could hang on to my legs.

VLADIMIR: And who'd hang on to mine?

ESTRAGON: True.

VLADIMIR: Show all the same. [*Estragon loosens the cord that holds up his trousers which, much too big for him, fall about his ankles. They look at the cord.*] It might do at a pinch. But is it strong enough?

ESTRAGON: We'll soon see. Here.

> *They each take an end of the cord and pull. It breaks. They almost fall.*

VLADIMIR: Not worth a curse.

> *Silence.*

ESTRAGON: You say we have to come back tomorrow?

VLADIMIR: Yes.

ESTRAGON: Then we can bring a good bit of rope.

VLADIMIR: Yes.

> *Silence.*

ESTRAGON: Didi.

VLADIMIR: Yes.

ESTRAGON: I can't go on like this.

VLADIMIR: That's what you think.

ESTRAGON: If we parted? That might be better for us.

VLADIMIR: We'll hang ourselves tomorrow. [*Pause.*] Unless Godot comes.

ESTRAGON: And if he comes?

VLADIMIR: We'll be saved.

POINTS FOR DISCUSSION

1. Beckett, when asked who or what he meant by Godot, said, 'If I knew, I would have said so in the play.' Is there anything in these extracts to support the view that Godot = God?

2. Beckett once said with regard to the theme of the play,[1] 'There is a wonderful sentence in Augustine... "Do not despair; one of the thieves was saved. Do not presume; one of the thieves was damned." ' What does Beckett seem to be saying about 'salvation' in these extracts (however inconclusively)?

3. A critic[2] has made this comment upon Beckett's plays as a whole, 'Not one of Beckett's people is able to accept either a religious or an atheistical position. Asked if they believe in God, they reply somewhat hesitantly "no", and then either curse him for not existing ("The bastard! He doesn't exist!") or alternatively curse him for the misery which he has fastened upon man. For the traditional faith in a "personal

[1] Harold Hobson, *International Theatre Annual No. 1* (1956).
[2] Richard N. Coe, *Beckett* (Writers and Critics, 1964).

God quaquaquaqua with white beard"[3] they seem at first to have nothing but contempt; yet on the other hand, they are spellbound by ... theological speculation.' How much of this do you see reflected in these extracts? How far does this inconsistency reflect some modern attitudes to religion? (Compare Alasdair MacIntyre's comment upon Tillich on page 120.)

4. The following is a quotation from a sermon by Paul Tillich,[4] a theologian with 'modern' views:

> Both the Old and the New Testaments describe our existence in relation to God as one of waiting... A religion in which that is forgotten, no matter how ecstatic or active or reasonable, replaces God by its own creation of an image of God. Our religious life is characterized more by that kind of creation than anything else. I think of the theologian who does not wait for God, because he possesses Him, enclosed within a doctrine ... of the churchman who does not wait for God, because he possesses Him, enclosed in an institution.... I am convinced that much of this rebellion against Christianity is due to the overt or veiled claim of the Christians to possess God, and, therefore, also, to the loss of this element of waiting, so decisive for the prophets and the apostles.... We have God through *not* having Him.

Do you agree with Tillich that 'much of this rebellion against Christianity is due to the... claim of the Christians to possess God'? To what extent do you see Tillich's ideas reflected in these extracts from *Waiting for Godot*?

5. '... a genuine religious quest in our age... an effort... in search of a dimension of the Ineffable.' (From *The Theatre of the Absurd* by Martin Esslin; see introduction, page 56.) Does anything in these extracts lead you to think that one could make this claim for *Waiting for Godot*?

[3] These words are spoken by Lucky in *Waiting for Godot* in his 'think'—a long monologue with only the barest thread of meaning running through it.

[4] Paul Tillich, *The Shaking of the Foundations* (Penguin, 1962).

8. CONSTANTINE CAVAFY

(a) WAITING FOR THE BARBARIANS (b) ITHAKA

CONSTANTINE CAVAFY was born in Alexandria in 1863. After his father's death, the family moved to England, where they stayed for seven years. Shortly afterwards, Cavafy spent three years in Constantinople, where he wrote his first poems, but eventually settled down again in Alexandria, and remained there for the rest of his life. As a young man he devoted himself to becoming a scholar, and spent many years studying Byzantine and Hellenic history, and also English, French, and Latin literature. In 1892, however, he took a job as a provisional clerk in the Ministry of Irrigation and held this somewhat incongruous post until his retirement thirty years later.

It was in the café life of Alexandria that Cavafy found his true satisfaction, surrounded by his friends and admirers, sipping Turkish coffee and talking endlessly on an enormous range of subjects. He wrote numerous poems, which he circulated among his friends, preserving only those which met with their approval. His first collection (of only fourteen poems) was published in 1904, and a second volume in 1910. Most of his work, however, was published in magazines, and a collected edition did not appear until 1935, two years after his death.

Although deeply conscious of the splendours of the classical tradition of Greece, Cavafy was much more drawn to the history of the wider Hellenistic world in the period after the decline of the empire of Alexander the Great, in particular to the great age of Alexandria in the third century B.C. and to the times of Constantine and later emperors, when Christianity became the official religion. It was a complex world of mingled races, religions, and cultures (Greek, Jewish, Christian, and Pagan), a world lacking in any obvious tragic or epic grandeur and which did not resound with many of the great names of history; it was upon this somewhat decadent, mildly disillusioned, hedonistic, and non-heroic world that Cavafy drew for the symbols and myths which gave shape and individuality to his ideas on life as he observed it in twentieth-century Alexandria. In its lack of drive and unity, and of a solid moral or religious foundation, he may have seen in that ancient world similarities to the world in which he lived.

E. M. Forster, who described Cavafy as 'one of the great poets of our time', summed up the paradoxical character of this intensely human and warm-hearted, and yet scholarly and detached figure in his picture of him as 'a Greek gentleman in a straw hat standing absolutely motionless at a slight angle to the universe'. To W. H. Auden he was a poet 'with a unique perspective of the world'. Cavafy's poetry is highly disciplined and may seem rather dry at first hearing; but it has a peculiar integrity and strength which derives from its very tautness and restraint.

Waiting for the Barbarians is a poem of great subtlety, capable of bearing a number of interpretations. A city awaits with eager expectation the arrival of the barbarians. We are not told very much about these barbarians, and the object of their visit is left vague, but certainly the rulers of the city were aiming to impress them and to appease them (and there is a hint that the control of the city was to be handed over to, or taken over by, them). The city waits from early morning until nightfall, but no barbarians arrive. The latter part of the poem introduces a deeper sense of mystery; it seems that, so far from merely failing to turn up, barbarians simply do not exist any more. The arrival of the barbarians was to be some kind of crisis which would act as a temporary solution to the problems of the city, and when the crisis fails to materialize, it is left unhappy and bewildered.

The second poem takes its title from the island home of Odysseus, the Greek hero who fought in the Trojan war; his journey home at the end of the war was long and full of hazards.

(a) *Waiting For the Barbarians*

What are we waiting for, gathered in the market-place?

   The barbarians are to arrive today.

Why so little activity in the senate?
Why do the senators sit there without legislating?

   Because the barbarians will arrive today.
   What laws should the senators make now?
   The barbarians, when they come, will do the legislating.

Why has our emperor risen so early,
and why does he sit at the largest gate of the city
on the throne, in state, wearing the crown?

Because the barbarians will arrive today.
And the emperor is waiting to receive
their leader. He has even prepared
a parchment for him. There
he has given him many titles and names.

Why did our two consuls and our praetors go out
today in the scarlet, the embroidered, togas?
Why did they wear bracelets with so many amethysts,
and rings with brilliant sparkling emeralds?
Why today do they carry precious staves
splendidly inlaid with silver and gold?

Because the barbarians will arrive today;
and such things dazzle barbarians.

And why don't the worthy orators come as always
to make their speeches, say what they have to say?

Because the barbarians will arrive today;
and they are bored by eloquence and public speaking.

What does this sudden uneasiness mean,
and this confusion? (How grave the faces have become!)
Why are the streets and squares rapidly emptying,
and why is everyone going back home so lost in thought?

Because it is night and the barbarians have not come.
And some men have arrived from the frontiers
and they say that barbarians don't exist any longer.

And now, what will become of us without barbarians?
They were a kind of solution.

POINTS FOR DISCUSSION

1. Describe as fully as possible what seems to be the attitude of the citizens towards the barbarians. How did they expect the barbarians to react?
2. How do you interpret the reactions of the citizens to the failure of the barbarians to arrive?

3. In what ways do you think that the barbarians would have been 'a kind of solution'? What do you think were the problems of the citizens which needed solving? What comment do you think this poem is making on order and affluence?

4. Do you see any similarities between this poem and any other extracts in this book which are concerned with the theme of waiting?

(b) *Ithaka*

When you set out for Ithaka
ask that your way be long,
full of adventure, full of instruction.
The Laistrygonians and the Cyclops,
angry Poseidon—do not fear them:
such as these you will never find
as long as thought is lofty, as long as a rare
emotion touch your spirit and your body.
The Laistrygonians and the Cyclops,
angry Poseidon—you will not meet them
unless you carry them in your soul,
unless your soul raise them up before you.

Ask that your way be long.
At many a summer dawn to enter
—with what gratitude, what joy—
ports seen for the first time;
to stop at Phoenician trading centres,
and to buy good merchandise,
mother of pearl and coral, amber and ebony,
and sensuous perfumes of every kind,
sensuous perfumes as lavishly as you can;
to visit many Egyptian cities,
to gather stores of knowledge from the learned.

Have Ithaka always in your mind.
Your arrival there is what you are destined for.
But don't in the least hurry the journey.
Better it last for years,
so that when you reach the island you are old,
rich with all that you have gained on the way,
not expecting Ithaka to give you wealth.

Ithaka gave you the splendid journey.
Without her you would not have set out.
She hasn't anything else to give you.
And if you find her poor, Ithaka hasn't deceived you.
So wise have you become, of such experience,
that already you'll have understood what these Ithakas mean.

POINTS FOR DISCUSSION

1. Sum up the attitude to life which is expressed in this poem. Does it seem to you to be optimistic and positive? Or pessimistic and negative?

2. What do you think that 'Ithaka' represents? In what ways is the idea of 'Ithaka' important?

3. Throughout his life Cavafy regretted his inability to accept orthodox Christianity, particularly the belief in an after-life. Can you see any evidence in this poem of this ambivalent attitude towards Christianity?

9. MARC CONNELLY

GREEN PASTURES

MARC CONNELLY is an American dramatist. His best known play is *Green Pastures*, which won the Pulitzer Prize in 1930. The author says in his introductory note to the play that it is 'an attempt to present certain aspects of living religion in terms of its believers. The religion is that of thousands of Negroes of the Deep South. With terrific spiritual hunger and great humility ... (they) have adapted the contents of the Bible to the consistencies of their everyday lives.' The serious purpose behind this play is enough to exempt the author from the charge that he is describing the simple beliefs of the Negroes of the 1930s with condescension and amused superiority. Nevertheless, as is evident from this extract, there is a great deal of lively humour in the play; the image of God that it presents, for all its inadequacy to us, is a vigorous one, and alive.

Heaven, as represented in *Green Pastures,* is inhabited by Negro angels, archangels, and cherubs. God himself is the tallest and biggest; he wears 'a white shirt with a white bow tie, a long Prince Albert coat of black alpaca, black trousers and congress gaiters.' He makes his first appearance in the play at a fish fry which is taking place in pre-Creation Heaven. The extract which follows consists of the final three scenes of the play.

SCENE VI

GOD *is writing at his desk. Outside, past the door, goes* HOSEA, *a dignified old man, with wings like* JACOB'S. GOD, *sensing his presence, looks up from the paper he is examining, and follows him out of the corner of his eye. Angrily he resumes his work as soon as* HOSEA *is out of sight. There is a knock on the door.*

GOD: Who is it?
> GABRIEL *enters.*
GABRIEL: It's de delegation, Lawd.
GOD [*wearily*]: Tell 'em to come in.
> ABRAHAM, ISAAC, JACOB *and* MOSES *enter.*
Good mo'nin', gen'lemen.

THE VISITORS: Good mo'nin', Lawd.

GOD: What kin, I do for you?

MOSES: You know, Lawd. Go back to our people.

GOD [*shaking his head*]: Ev'ry day fo' hund'ed's of years you boys have come in to ask dat same thing. De answer is still de same. I repented of de people I made. I said I would deliver dem no more. Good mo'nin', gen'lemen.

The four VISITORS *rise and exeunt.* GABRIEL *remains.*

Gabe, why do dey do it?

GABRIEL: I 'spect dey think you gonter change yo' mind.

GOD [*sadly*]: Dey don' know me.

HOSEA *again passes the door. His shadow shows on wall.* GABRIEL *is perplexed, as he watches.* GOD *again looks surreptitiously over his shoulder at the passing figure.*

I don' like dat, either.

GABRIEL: What, Lawd?

GOD: Dat man.

GABRIEL: He's jest a prophet, Lawd. Dat's jest old Hosea. He jest come up the other day.

GOD: I know. He's one of de few dat's come up yere since I was on de earth last time.

GABRIEL: Ain' been annoyin' you, has he?

GOD: I don' like him walkin' past de door.

GABRIEL: All you got to do is tell him to stop, Lawd.

GOD: Yes, I know. I don' want to tell him. He's got a right up yere or he wouldn' be yere.

GABRIEL: You needn' be bothered by him hangin' aroun' de office all de time. I'll tell 'im. Who's he think he——

GOD: No, Gabe. I find it ain' in me to stop him. I sometimes jest wonder why he don' come in and say hello.

GABRIEL: You want him to do dat? [*He moves as if to go to the door.*]

GOD: He never has spoke to me, and if he don' wanta come in, I ain't gonter make him. But dat ain't de worst of it, Gabriel.

GABRIEL: What is, Lawd?

GOD: Ev'y time he goes past de door I hears a voice.

GABRIEL: One of de angels?

GOD [*shaking his head*]: It's from de earth. It's a man.

GABRIEL: You mean he's prayin'?

GOD: No, he ain' exactly prayin'. He's jest talkin' in such a way dat I got to lissen. His name is Hezdrel.

GABRIEL: Is he on de books?

GOD: No, not yet. But ev'y time dat Hosea goes past I hear dat voice.

GABRIEL: Den tell *it* to stop.

GOD: I find I don' wanta do that, either. Dey's gettin' ready to take Jerusalem down dere. Dat was my big fine city. Dis Hezdrel, he's jest one of de defenders. [*Suddenly and passionately, almost wildly.*] I ain' comin' down. You hear me? I ain' comin' down. [*He looks at* GABRIEL.] Go ahead, Gabriel. 'Tend to yo' chores. I'm gonter keep wukkin' yere.

GABRIEL: I hates to see you feelin' like dis, Lawd.

GOD: Dat's all right. Even bein' Gawd ain't a bed of roses.

> GABRIEL *exits.* HOSEA'S *shadow is on the wall. For a second* HOSEA *hesitates.* GOD *looks at the wall. Goes to window.*

I hear you. I know yo' fightin' bravely, but I ain' coming down. Oh, why don' you leave me alone? You know you ain' talkin' to me. *Is* you talkin' to me? I can't stand yo' talkin' dat way. I kin only hear part of what you' sayin', and it puzzles me. Don' you know you cain't puzzle God? [*A pause. Then tenderly.*] Do you want me to come down dere ve'y much? You know I said I wouldn't come down? [*Fiercely*]. Why don' he answer me a little? [*With clenched fists, looks down through the window.*] Listen! I'll tell you what I'll do. I ain' goin' to promise you anythin', and I ain' goin' to do nothin' to help you. I'm jest feelin' a little low, an' I'm only comin' down to make myself feel a little better, dat's all.

> The stage is darkened. CHOIR *begins 'A Blind Man Stood in De Middle of De Road', and continues until the lights go up on the next scene.*

SCENE VII

It is a shadowed corner beside the walls of the temple in Jerusalem. The light of camp fires flickers on the figure of HEZDREL, *who was* ADAM *in Part I. He stands in the same position* ADAM *held when first discovered but in his right hand is a sword, and his left is in a sling. Around him are several prostrate bodies. Pistol and cannon shots, then a trumpet call. Six young* MEN *enter from left in command of a* CORPORAL. *They are all armed.*

CORPORAL: De fightin's stopped fo' de night, Hezdrel.

HEZDREL: Yes?

CORPORAL: Dey're goin' to begin ag'in at cockcrow.

    MAN *enters, crosses the stage and exits.*

Herod say he's goin' to take de temple tomorrow, burn de books and de Ark of de Covenant, and put us all to de sword.

HEZDREL: Yo' ready, ain't you?

EVERYBODY: Yes, Hezdrel.

HEZDREL: Did de food get in through de hole in de city wall?

    Two SOLDIERS *enter, cross the stage and exit.*

CORPORAL: Yessuh, we's goin' back to pass it out now.

HEZDREL: Good. Any mo' of our people escape today?

CORPORAL: Ol' Herod's got de ol' hole covered up now, but fifteen of our people got out a new one we made.

    Other SOLDIERS *enter, cross the stage and exit.*

HEZDREL: Good. Take dese yere wounded men back and git 'em took care of.

CORPORAL: Yes, suh.

    They pick up the bodies on the ground and carry them off-stage as HEZDREL *speaks.*

HEZDREL: So dey gonter take de temple in de mo'nin'? We'll be waitin' for 'em. Jest remember, boys, when dey kill us we leap out of our skins, right into de lap of God.

    The men disappear with the wounded; from the deep shadow upstage comes GOD.

GOD: Hello, Hezdrel—Adam.

HEZDREL [*rubbing his forehead*]: Who is you?

GOD: Me? I'm jest an ol' preacher, from back in de hills.

HEZDREL: What you doin' yere?

GOD: I heard you boys was fightin'. I jest wanted to see how it was goin'.

HEZDREL: Well, it ain't goin' so well.

GOD: Dey got you skeered, huh?

HEZDREL: Look yere, who is you, a spy in my brain?

GOD: Cain't you see I'se one of yo' people?

HEZDREL: Listen, Preacher, we ain't skeered. We's gonter be killed, but we ain't skeered.

GOD: I'se glad to hear dat. Kin I ask you a question, Hezdrel?

HEZDREL: What is it?

GOD: How is it you is so brave?

HEZDREL: Caize we got faith, dat's why!

GOD: Faith? In who?

HEZDREL: In our dear Lawd God.

GOD: But God say he abandoned ev'y one down yere.

HEZDREL: Who say dat? Who dare say dat of de Lawd God of Hosea?

GOD: De God of Hosea?

HEZDREL: You heard me. Look yere, you *is* a spy in my brain!

GOD: No, I ain', Hezdrel. I'm jest puzzled. You ought to know dat.

HEZDREL: How come you so puzzled 'bout de God of Hosea?

GOD: I don' know. Maybe I jest don' hear things. You see, I live 'way back in de hills.

HEZDREL: What you wanter find out?

GOD: Ain' de God of Hosea de same Jehovah dat was de God of Moses?

HEZDREL [*contemptuously*]: No. Dat ol' God of wrath and vengeance? We have de God dat Hosea preached to us. He's de one God.

GOD: Who's he?

HEZDREL [*reverently*]: De God of mercy.

GOD: Hezdrel, don' you think dey must be de same God?

HEZDREL: I don't know. I ain't bothered to think much about it. Maybe dey is. Maybe our God is de same ol' God. I guess we jest got tired of his appearance dat ol' way.

GOD: What you mean, Hezdrel?

HEZDREL: Oh, dat ol' God dat walked de earth in de shape of a man. I guess he lived wid man so much dat all he seen was de sins in man. Dat's what made him de God of wrath and vengeance. Co'se he made Hosea. An' Hosea never would 'a' found what mercy was unless dere was a little of it in God, too. Anyway, he ain't a fearsome God no mo'. Hosea showed us dat.

GOD: How you s'pose Hosea found dat mercy?

HEZDREL: De only way he could find it. De only way I found it. De only way anyone kin find it.

GOD: How's dat?

HEZDREL: Through sufferin'.

GOD [*after a pause*]. What if dey kill you in de mo'nin', Hezdrel?

HEZDREL: If dey do, dey do. Dat's all.

GOD: Herod say he's goin' to burn de temple——

HEZDREL: So he say.

GOD: And burn de Ark an' de books. Den dat's de end of de books, ain' it?

HEZDREL [*buoyantly*]. What you mean? If he burns dem things in dere? Naw. Dem's jest copies.

GOD: Where is de others?

HEZDREL [*tapping his head*]: Dey's a set in yere. Fifteen got out through de hole in de city wall today. A hundred and fifty got out durin' de week. Each of 'em is a set of de books. Dey's scattered safe all over de countryside now, jest waitin' to git pen and paper fo' to put 'em down ag'in.

GOD [*proudly*]: Dey cain't lick you, kin dey, Hezdrel?

HEZDREL [*smiling*]: I know dey cain't. [*Trumpet.*] You better get out o' yere, Preacher, if you wanter carry de news to yo' people. It'll soon be daylight.

GOD: I'm goin'. [*He takes a step upstage and stops.*] Want me to take any message?

HEZDREL: Tell de people in de hills dey ain't nobody like de Lawd God of Hosea.

GOD: I will. If dey kill you tomorrow I'll bet dat God of Hosea'll be waitin' for you.

HEZDREL: I *know* he will.

GOD [*quietly*]. Thank you, Hezdrel.

HEZDREL: Fo' what?

GOD: Fo' tellin me so much. You see I been so far away, I guess I was jest way behin' de times.

> *He exits. Pause, then trumpet sounds.*
>
> HEZDREL *paces back and forth once or twice. Another young* SOLDIER *appears. Other* MEN *enter and stand grouped about* HEZDREL.

SECOND OFFICER [*excitedly*]: De cock's jest crowed, Hezdrel. Dey started de fightin' ag'in.

HEZDREL: We's ready for 'em. Come on, boys.

> *From the darkness upstage comes another group of* SOLDIERS.

Dis is de day dey say dey'll git us. Le's fight till de last man goes. What d'you say?

CORPORAL. Le's go, Hezdrel!

HEZDREL [*calling left*]: Give 'em ev'ything, boys!

> *There is a movement toward the left, a bugle call and the sound of distant battle. The lights go out. The* CHOIR *is heard singing 'March On', triumphantly. They continue to sing after the lights go up on the next scene.*

SCENE VIII

It is the same setting as the Fish Fry Scene in Part I. The same ANGELS *are present but the* CHOIR, *instead of marching, is standing in a double row on an angle upstage right.* GOD *is seated in an armchair near centre. He faces the audience. As the* CHOIR *continues to sing,* GABRIEL *enters, unnoticed by the chattering angels. He looks at* GOD *who is staring thoughtfully toward the audience.*

GABRIEL: You look a little pensive, Lawd.

GOD *nods his head.*

Have a seegar, Lawd?

GOD: No thanks, Gabriel.

GABRIEL *goes to the table, accepts a cup of custard; chats with the* ANGEL *behind the table for a moment as he sips, puts the cup down and returns to the side of* GOD.

GABRIEL: You look awful pensive, Lawd. You been sittin' yere, lookin' dis way, an awful long time. Is it somethin' serious, Lawd?

GOD: Very serious, Gabriel.

GABRIEL [*awed by his tone*]: Lawd, is de time come for me to blow?

GOD: Not yet, Gabriel. I'm just thinkin'.

GABRIEL: What about, Lawd? [*Puts up hand. Singing stops.*]

GOD: 'Bout somethin' de boy tol' me. Somethin' 'bout Hosea, and himself. How dey foun' somethin'.

GABRIEL: What, Lawd?

GOD: Mercy. [*A pause.*] Through sufferin', he said.

GABRIEL: Yes, Lawd.

GOD: I'm tryin' to find it, too. It's awful impo'tant. It's awful impo'tant to all de people on my earth. Did he mean dat even God must suffer?

GOD *continues to look out over the audience for a moment and than a look of surprise comes into his face. He sighs. In the distance a voice cries.*

THE VOICE: Oh, look at him! Oh, look dey goin' to make him carry it up dat high hill! Dey goin' to nail him to it! Oh, dat's a terrible burden for one man to carry!

GOD *rises and murmurs 'Yes!' as if in recognition. The* HEAVENLY BEINGS *have been watching him closely, and now,*

seeing him smile gently, draw back, relieved. All the ANGELS
burst into 'Hallelujah, King Jesus'. GOD *continues to smile
as the lights fade away. The singing becomes fortissimo.*

CURTAIN

POINTS FOR DISCUSSION

1. It has been said that we will inevitably reject this Negro mythology
either with 'superiority and scorn or with kindly understanding and
sympathy'. What is your reaction?

2. 'The inescapable fact is that we cannot feel or think except anthropomorphically.' Discuss what is meant by 'anthropomorphically'. In
what ways are our own images of God outmoded? To what extent are
we influenced by images of God held over from our childhood?

3. 'An' Hosea never would 'a' found what mercy was unless dere was
a little of it in God too.' Discuss the implications of this remark.

4. 'Behind the naivete of "de Lawd's" remark that he was "just way
behin' de times" lies a truth which is highly relevant to the presenta-
tion of Christianity today.' Discuss this comment.

5. Someone once said that he thought of God as an 'oblong blur'. Is
this sort of predicament the only alternative to an anthropomorphic
image? What should be our attitude to images of God?

10. SAMUEL BUTLER

EREWHON

SAMUEL BUTLER (1835–1902) was born at Langar in Nottinghamshire. Both his father and grandfather were clergymen. and it was expected that he too would enter the ministry in his turn. But after he had taken his degree in classics at Cambridge, his highly independent spirit rebelled against the Church and against the suffocating moral atmosphere of the home in which he had been brought up; he broke with his father and emigrated to New Zealand, renouncing Christianity. After some success as a sheep farmer, he returned to England in 1864 and devoted himself to a very wide range of interests; apart from writing about sixteen full length books, he was also an artist and exhibited at the Royal Academy.

Erewhon, from which these extracts are taken, is a satire on life and attitudes in England at that time, and, like Gulliver's Travels, takes the form of a journey in a mysterious and imaginary land. The institutions of Erewhon are partly Utopian, and partly—as is implied by the name Nosnibor—satirical inversions of those in Victorian England.

Butler was a born protester, and found it difficult to resist attacking any generally accepted or fashionable belief, whether Christian, agnostic, or scientific; as a result, inconsistencies of attitude abound in his writings. His account of the Musical Banks, however, is an extremely clever parody, behind which can be detected a convincing picture of the attitudes of those times.

(a) *A visit to one of the Musical Banks with Mrs. Nosnibor and her daughters*

The ladies were just putting away their work and preparing to go out. I asked them where they were going. They answered with a certain air of reserve that they were going to the bank to get some money.

Now I had already collected that the mercantile affairs of the Erewhonians were conducted on a totally different system from our own; I had, however, gathered little hitherto, except that they had two distinct commercial systems, of which the one appealed more strongly to the imagination than anything to which we are accustomed in Europe, inasmuch as the banks that were conducted upon this system were decorated in the most profuse fashion, and all mercantile transactions were accompanied with music, so that they were called Musical Banks, though the music was hideous to a European ear.

As for the system itself I never understood it, neither can I do so now; they have a code in connection with it which I have not the slightest doubt that they understand, but no foreigner can hope to do so. One rule runs into, and against, another as in a most complicated grammar, or as in a Chinese pronunciation, wherein I am told that the slightest change in accentuation or tone of voice alters the meaning of a whole sentence. Whatever is incoherent in my description must be referred to the fact of my never having attained to a full comprehension of the subject.

So far, however, as I could collect anything certain, I gathered that they have two distinct currencies, each under the control of its own banks and mercantile codes. One of these (the one with the Musical Banks) was supposed to be *the* system, and to give out the currency in which all monetary transactions should be carried on; and as far as I could see, all who wished to be considered respectable, kept a larger or smaller balance at these banks. On the other hand, if there is one thing of which I am more sure than another, it is that the amount so kept had no direct commercial value in the outside world; I am sure that the managers and cashiers of the Musical Banks were not paid in their own currency. Mr. Nosnibor used to go to these banks, or rather to the great mother bank of the city, sometimes but not very often. He was a pillar of one of the other kind of banks, though he appeared to hold some minor office also in the musical ones. The ladies generally went alone; as indeed was the case in most families, except on state occasions.

I had long wanted to know more of this strange system, and had the greatest desire to accompany my hostess and her daughters. I had seen them go out almost every morning since my arrival and had noticed that they carried their purses in their hands, not exactly ostentatiously, yet just so as that those who met them should see whither they were going. I had never, however, yet been asked to go with them myself.

It is not easy to convey a person's manner by words, and I can hardly give any idea of the peculiar feeling that came upon me when I saw the ladies on the point of starting for the bank. There was a something of regret, a something as though they would wish to take me with them, but did not like to ask me, and yet as though I were hardly to ask to be taken. I was determined, however, to bring matters to an issue with my hostess about my going with them, and after a little parleying, and many inquiries as to whether I was perfectly sure that I myself wished to go, it was decided that I might do so.... We crossed the sward and entered the building. If the outside had been impressive the inside was even more so. It was very lofty and divided into several parts by walls which rested upon massive pillars; the windows were filled with stained glass descriptive of the principal commercial incidents of the bank for many ages. In a remote part of the building there were men and boys singing; this was the only disturbing feature, for as the gamut was still unknown, there was no music in the country which could be agreeable to a European ear. The singers seemed to have derived their inspirations from the songs of birds and the wailing of the wind, which last they tried to imitate in melancholy cadences that at times degenerated into a howl. To my thinking the noise was hideous, but it produced a great effect upon my companions, who professed themselves much moved. As soon as the singing was over, the ladies requested me to stay where I was while they went inside the place from which it had seemed to come.

During their absence certain reflections forced themselves upon me.

In the first place, it struck me as strange that the building should be so nearly empty; I was almost alone, and the few besides myself had been led by curiosity, and had no intention of doing business with the bank. But there might be more inside. I stole up to the curtain, and ventured to draw the extreme edge of it on one side. No, there was hardly any one there. I saw a large number of cashiers, all at their desks ready to pay cheques, and one or two who seemed to be the managing partners. I also saw my hostess and her daughters and two or three other ladies; also three or four old women and the boys from one of the neighbouring Colleges of Unreason; but there was no one else. This did not look at though the bank was doing a very large business; and yet I had always been told that every one in the city dealt with this establishment....

They soon joined me. For some few minutes we all kept silence, but at last I ventured to remark that the bank was not so busy to-day as it probably often was. On this Mrs. Nosnibor said that it was indeed melancholy to see what little heed people paid to the most precious of all institutions. I could say nothing in reply, but I have ever been of opinion that the greater part of mankind do approximately know where they get that which does them good.

Mrs. Nosnibor went on to say that I must not think there was any want of confidence in the bank because I had seen so few people there; the heart of the country was thoroughly devoted to these establishments, and any sign of their being in danger would bring in support from the most unexpected quarters. It was only because people knew them to be so very safe that in some cases (as she lamented to say in Mr. Nosnibor's) they felt that their support was unnecessary. Moreover, these institutions never departed from the safest and most approved banking principles. Thus they never allowed interest on deposit, a thing now frequently done by certain bubble companies, which by doing an illegitimate trade had drawn many customers away; and even the shareholders were fewer than formerly, owing to the innovations of these unscrupulous persons, for the Musical Banks paid little or no dividend, but divided their profits by way of bonus on the original shares once in every thirty thousand years; and as it was now only two thousand years since there had been one of these distributions people felt that they could not hope for another in their own time and preferred investments whereby they got some more tangible return; all of which, she said, was very melancholy to think of.

Having made these last admissions, she returned to her original statement, namely, that every one in the country really supported these banks.

POINTS FOR DISCUSSION

1. Explain what Butler means by the 'two distinct currencies'.
2. '... all who wished to be considered respectable kept a larger or smaller balance at these banks.' What particular attitude to religion is Butler satirizing here? To what extent does this attitude persist today?
3. What other aspects of the religious attitudes of the Victorians is he satirizing?

4. What can you learn about church attendance in Victorian times from Butler's satirical account? To what extent would he have altered it if he had written it in the present day?

(b)   The coinage of the Musical Banks; reflections on religion in general

She might say what she pleased, but her manner carried no conviction, and later on I saw signs of general indifference to these banks that were not to be mistaken. Their supporters often denied it, but the denial was generally so couched as to add another proof of its existence. In commercial panics, and in times of general distress, the people as a mass did not so much as even think of turning to these banks. A few might do so, some from habit and early training, some from the instinct that prompts us to catch at any straw when we think ourselves drowning, but few from a genuine belief that the Musical Banks could save them from financial ruin if they were unable to meet their engagements in the other kind of currency.

In conversation with one of the Musical Bank managers I ventured to hint this as plainly as politeness would allow. He said that it had been more or less true till lately, but that now they had put fresh stained-glass windows into all the banks in the country, and repaired the buildings, and enlarged the organs; the presidents, moreover, had taken to riding in omnibuses and talking nicely to people in the streets, and to remembering the ages of their children, and giving them things when they were naughty, so that all would henceforth go smoothly.

'But haven't you done anything to the money itself?' said I timidly.

'It is not necessary,' he rejoined; 'not in the least necessary, I assure you.'

And yet any one could see that the money given out at these banks was not that with which people bought their bread, meat, and clothing. It was like it at a first glance, and was stamped with designs that were often of great beauty; it was not, again, a spurious coinage, made with the intention that it should be mistaken for the money in actual use; it was more like a toy money, or the counters used for certain games at cards; for, notwithstanding the beauty of the designs, the material on which they were stamped was as nearly valueless as possible. Some were covered with tinfoil, but the greater part were frankly of a cheap base metal the exact nature of which I was not able to determine. Indeed they were made of a great variety of metals, or, perhaps more accurately, alloys, some of which were hard, while others would bend easily and assume almost any form which their possessor might desire at the moment.

Of course every one knew that their commercial value was *nil*, but all those who wished to be considered respectable thought it incumbent upon them to retain a few coins in their possession, and to let them be seen from time to time in their hands and purses. Not only this, but they would stick to it that the current coin of the realm was dross in comparison with the Musical Bank coinage. Perhaps, however, the strangest thing of all was that these very people would at times make fun in small ways of the whole system; indeed, there was hardly any insinuation against it which they would not tolerate and even applaud in their daily newspapers if written anonymously, while if the same thing were said without ambiguity to their faces—nominative case, verb and accusative being all in their right places, and doubt impossible—they would consider themselves very seriously and justly outraged, and accuse the speaker of being unwell.

I never could understand (neither can I quite do so now, though I begin to see better what they mean) why a single currency should not suffice them; it would seem to me as though all their dealings would have been thus greatly simplified; but I was met with a look of horror if ever I dared to hint at it. Even those who to my certain knowledge kept only just enough money at the Musical Banks to swear by, would call the other banks (where their securities really lay) cold, deadening, paralysing, and the like.

. . . .

Yet we do something not so very different from this even in England, and as regards the dual commercial system, all countries have, and have had, a law of the land, and also another law, which, though professedly more sacred, has far less effect on their daily life and actions. It seems as though the need for some law over and above, and sometimes even conflicting with, the law of the land, must spring from something that lies deep down in man's nature; indeed, it is hard to think that man could ever have become man at all, but for the gradual evolution of a perception that though this world looms so large when we are in it, it may seem a little thing when we have got away from it.

When man had grown to the perception that in the everlasting Is-and-Is-Not of nature, the world and all that it contains, including man, is at the same time both seen and unseen, he felt the need of two rules of life, one for the seen, and the other for the unseen side of things. For the laws affecting the seen world he claimed the sanction of seen powers; for the unseen (of which he knows nothing save that it exists and is powerful) he appealed to the unseen power (of which, again, he knows nothing save that it exists and is powerful) to which he gives the name of God.

Some Erewhonian opinions concerning the intelligence of the unborn embryo, that I regret my space will not permit me to lay before the reader, have led me to conclude that the Erewhonian Musical Banks, and perhaps the religious systems of all countries, are now more or less of an attempt to uphold the unfathomable and unconscious instinctive wisdom of millions of past generations, against the comparatively shallow, consciously reasoning, and ephemeral conclusions drawn from that of the last thirty or forty.

The saving feature of the Erewhonian Musical Bank system (as distinct from the quasi-idolatrous views which co-exist with it, and on which I will touch later) was that while it bore witness to the existence of a kingdom that is not of this world, it made no attempt to pierce the veil that hides it from human eyes. It is here that almost all religions go wrong. Their priests try to make us believe that they know more about the unseen world than those whose eyes are still blinded by the seen, can ever know—forgetting that while to deny the existence of an unseen kingdom is bad, to pretend that we know more about it than its bare existence is no better.

This chapter is already longer than I intended, but I should like to say that in spite of the saving feature of which I have just spoken, I cannot help thinking that the Erewhonians are on the eve of some great change in their religious opinions, or at any rate in that part of them which finds expression through their Musical Banks. So far as I could see, fully ninety per cent. of the population of the metropolis looked upon these banks with something not far removed from contempt. If this is so, any such startling event as is sure to arise sooner or later may serve as nucleus to a new order of things that will be more in harmony with both the heads and hearts of the people.

POINTS FOR DISCUSSION

1. 'But haven't you done anything to the money itself?' What is Butler attacking in his description of the coinage of the Musical Banks?

2. Discuss the comments Butler makes about religion in general in the last half of this extract.

3. Butler foresees 'some great change' in religious opinions. In the light of this remark, what do you think he would have to say about the present state of religious beliefs?

11. JOYCE CARY

THE CAPTIVE AND THE FREE

JOYCE CARY was born in Londonderry in 1888 and educated at Clifton College and Trinity College, Oxford. He served in the British Red Cross in the Balkan War from 1912 to 1913, and in 1914 he entered the Colonial Service in Nigeria. He did war service with the Nigerian army and afterwards returned to his career as a District Officer until 1920, when he retired on health grounds. He then settled down in England to a career of writing, his first novel, *Aissa Saved*, being published in 1932.

The Captive and the Free was written during the last three years of his life, while he was dying from muscular dystrophy. He said of it: 'It will break my heart if I don't finish this.' He did in fact complete it sufficiently for it to be published after his death in 1957, when it had been carefully edited by Winifred Davin.

Cary once said, 'Twice in my life I have nearly been caught by the Church but thank God both times I have managed to save my soul.' This remark well illustrates the unorthodox and protestant nature of his beliefs. But his rejection of orthodoxy did not lead him, unlike so many of his literary contemporaries, into nihilism and despair. He had an intensely strong conviction of some ultimate spiritual reality, of the power of human love and of the joy in creating. His characters frequently express this positive and creative joy in life, whether it is the Nigerian clerk in *Mister Johnson* or the wildly eccentric artist, Gully Jimson, in *The Horse's Mouth;* he was drawn to unconventional and even cranky characters, whom he uses in his novels to illuminate various aspects of human life. Lord David Cecil says of him in his introduction to this novel:

> As he saw it, the rogue and the freak were just as likely to have an insight into truth as were the correct and the respectable... this is true of *The Captive and the Free*. Here the subject is religion. Preedy, the main character, is a faith healer who runs a shabby little tabernacle in London. The respectable churches look askance at him as a charlatan and man of bad character, who had been converted as a result of seducing a girl of fourteen with whom he still has intermittent relations. But in fact his whole life is dominated by a pure intuitional faith in God, which never fails him whatever his failures or misfortunes. Contrasted with him is

Syson, an Anglican clergyman who believes Preedy to be a fraud. His efforts to expose him lead him to search into his own beliefs more deeply than ever before, with the result that he loses his orthodox faith and breaks with the Church. At the end he is left believing simply in the existence of a divine beneficent spirit which it is man's duty to worship. Both these are free spirits boldly following the call of their hearts and souls without reference to other people's opinion. So also is Alice, the girl in Preedy's life. The rest are in some degree what Cary calls captives: people who, for good or bad reasons, feel themselves compelled to accept standards and religious views inherited or imposed on them by society. But captive and free alike are conceived primarily in their relation to religious truth. Everyone, consciously or not, is represented as seeking salvation.

Cary presents his scene with an impersonal justice that leaves his own attitude enigmatic. There is no doubt he thinks that Preedy's religion is the real thing; but whether or not his successful miracles are explicable on rational grounds, Cary does not tell us. Syson's faith has not the pure intensity of Preedy's, and he is wrong in thinking Preedy a fraud. But he is the more virtuous and intelligent man of the two, and his own final views are stated with sympathy.

In fact—though he is vigilantly careful to give no hints of this in the book—they are close to Cary's own. Cary was a profoundly religious spirit of that intensely individual and protestant kind which cannot find fulfilment in any corporate body; he had to carve out his creed by himself and for himself. Brought up as an orthodox Anglican, he lost all religious faith in early manhood to find a new one in mature life. It was not orthodox; it was not Christian in any substantial sense. Cary did not identify God with Christ or with any kind of personal spirit. But experience had convinced him that man's apprehension of beauty and of human love was inexplicable on any purely rational or materialist terms. It was proof of some transcendental spiritual reality with which a man must relate harmoniously if he is to find satisfaction. He did not hold this as a mere pious opinion. It burned within him, an intuitive conviction as strong as that of Preedy, strengthening his spirit and directing his actions. To be often in his company was to be aware of its presence. This strong faith was what enabled him at the end against appalling odds to win his tragic race with death.

*(a) Syson is the curate of St. Enoch's, in the parish of
which is the Pant's Road Mission of Faith and Re-
generation run by the faith-healer called Preedy who
is referred to in the introduction. Syson, who at
this stage is still 'captive' to beliefs which he later
finds he cannot adhere to, has made some outspoken
criticisms of Preedy's honesty and morals (he had
called him 'a crook on the make') and is eventually
sued for slander. The following extract describes his
cross-examination*

Cross-examined, he agreed at once that he had described Preedy
as a hypocrite and a liar.

Counsel then asked, 'Did you wish to drive Mr. Preedy and his
Mission out of your parish?'

'I wished to warn members of my church against the Mission.'

'Because members of the church preferred it?'

'No, because it was teaching lies.'

'How did you describe it, as a racket?'

'Yes, I certainly did.'

'By racket, meaning swindle, fraud, run for profit?'

'Not exactly. Preedy may believe in it himself.'

'But you said he was teaching lies.'

'He might believe in the lies.'

'Do you really tell the court that that it what you meant by
racket?'

'These people live in a fog.'

'Please answer my question.'

'Perhaps they think they have a right to deceive people.'

'I see—you say Preedy deliberately chooses to deceive.'

'No, exaggerate.'

'You say he tells lies—do you mean that?'

'He may think it right to do so.'

'Please answer my question.'

Syson coloured and said angrily, 'I'm trying to explain that he
might think it right to express a confidence he didn't feel. I'm
giving him the benefit of the doubt.'

'You still haven't answered my question.'

'But I'm answering——'

Here the judge intervened with some sharpness to tell Syson to answer Counsel's questions. What annoyed Syson was that he was not only trying to give the truth, but one favourable to Preedy. He was using, deliberately, a Christian charity towards the man. Like most people unused to legal procedure he did not understand the principle of examination. He thought it was meant to get truth directly and as much of it as possible. He had no idea of the complicated rules of advocacy. From the moment of the judge's rebuke he began to lose his temper.

Counsel then repeated his question and Syson answered, sharply, 'No.'

'And that's why you call the Mission a racket.'

'Yes, it promises what it can't perform.'

'Do you know that Mr. Preedy has cured hundreds of people of grave diseases? We have had two witnesses who were cured when doctors had given them up.'

'Blindness is a common neurosis and everyone over sixty who has a pain thinks it's cancer.'

'Do you believe that miracles are impossible?'

'No.'

'Did you preach a sermon in recent weeks declaring it was unnecessary to believe the Bible stories of miracles?'

'Not all of them, for instance, the miracle of the loaves and fishes.'

'You choose what to believe?'

'The resurrection is necessary to believe for any Christian.'

'It's a matter of choice?'

'If you don't believe the resurrection you couldn't call yourself a Christian.'

'Please answer—is it a matter of choice?'

'Yes.'

'Who chooses?'

'It's the general opinion of modern churchmen that——'

'I asked who chooses? Did you choose for yourself?'

'Yes.'

'Why?'

'I just don't find some of the stories credible. And they aren't necessary either.'

'You choose to believe that the Bible tells lies?'

'No—but not a factual truth.'

'You've just told us you couldn't believe in all the miracle stories.'

'One can accept them as religious truth.'

'Do you mean religious truth can involve telling factual lies?'

But it's unnecessary to give all the cross-examination; counsel had no difficulty in making Syson say that he did not believe in the Bible or the Articles, that he believed only what suited his personal fancy. And it is very doubtful if any Bishop would have done better in a witness box. He was then asked if he had signed the Articles in which he did not believe and if it was not hypocrisy to do so.

'So that you accuse Mr. Preedy of hypocrisy although he does believe exactly as he professes?'

'I say he couldn't do miracles. It's blasphemous to imagine it of a man of his character.'

'You think Mr. Preedy unfit to be a minister?'

'That's what I'm saying all the time.'

'You wanted to stop his work in your parish?'

'Everywhere and anywhere.'

Syson was now enraged and disgusted; he was only anxious to get away from this court and all its foolish prevaricating tricks. As for Preedy, it was already established that he was a man of the lowest character, actually a criminal. What was the good of all this talk?

This was why he grew so impatient at last and was easily led to declare that, yes, Preedy was a crook and he had wanted to drive him out of the parish and put an end to his mission.

POINTS FOR DISCUSSION

1. Asked if he believes that the Bible tells lies, Syson answers, 'No—but not a factual truth.' What is the point of the distinction he makes?

2. In the cross-examination, Counsel asks, 'Do you mean religious truth can involve telling factual lies?' and Cary stops his account at this point. How would you deal with this question?

3. Cary comments, 'It is doubtful if any Bishop would have done better in a witness box.' To what extent do you think this is intended as a criticism of Bishops?

*(b) Syson is found guilty of slander and has to pay £500
damages. Outraged by this verdict, he at first refuses
to pay and is sent to prison for contempt; soon, however,
he is persuaded to pay the damages and he is released.
But he finds that the total sum he owes, because of
costs, is more than £3000 and he realizes he is bankrupt*

Syson understood his wife's feelings and even her difficulties;
he forgave her, but he could not bear her presence or her chatter.
She represented for him the whole force of the circumstances
which had inflicted an agony of rage and self-contempt upon
him. As he sat beside her, feeling her like a jailer, like a cunning
mistress who had tied him up in a net of obligation everywhere
yielding and everywhere unbreakable, he longed only to be alone.
He wanted to think. He had been asking himself what would be
his next move to destroy this crook Preedy, and to make people
realize his wickedness. But all the time he was aware that there
was some other problem to be dealt with, some other question
that needed an answer.

He went suddenly to the vicarage and resigned his curacy.
This was both a relief and a surprise to Parsloe. But he felt it his
duty, all the same, to point out how foolish and unnecessary it
was, and to urge Syson to stay with him; at least not to take such
decisive action on the spur of the moment.

'My dear chap,' he said, 'I know how you feel. But why take
this desperate step? You've done fine work here, and I don't
know where I'll find anyone to suit the parish so well—a parish
so mixed as this. What's the real trouble? You needn't think this
verdict is going to worry us—most people here are all on your
side. Or is it because you don't like my line about Preedy? In
that case, of course——'

'You've got to do what you think right,' Syson said.

'And so have you. I quite see that. But can't we carry on on
those terms?'

Syson made no answer for a moment. Then he said, 'I've been
reading Hutley about faith-healing. You know, the telepathic
effects of prayer and undoubted miracles. All the same, you must
consult the doctors.'

'It's a good book—it covers the ground pretty thoroughly.'

There was a short pause and then Syson muttered, 'I suppose so—but it's not very convincing.'

'What do you mean?'

'About those miracles.'

'Oh, that's as you look at it.'

But he was worried about this large, slow curate of his. He liked the man, though he considered him both stupid and obstinate, a bad combination in any church. He said at last, 'A man like Preedy can always get a start of us because he has a slogan— something quite simple that any fool can understand. But, as we know, things are not so simple.'

'No.'

The 'no' expressed a faint irony and the vicar, glad of any clue to the man's thoughts, said, 'They can't be so in the nature of things—I mean, things as they are.'

Syson said nothing to this. He was gazing at his toes while he slowly wagged one foot.

'You get all sorts in any church and they have all sorts of belief—from the most credulous.'

'Do you suppose Hutley believes his own stuff,' Syson said, 'or does he just want to hang on to his job?'

This startled Parsloe. He said cautiously, 'Do you know how I came into the Church?'

'From a college mission, wasn't it?'

'More or less. I helped at the mission—that was in the twenties. And of course, I was a good socialist, a bit of a prig, I dare say. Taught a class for the Fabians—it was down near the docks. Not a nice spot. But it seemed to me that the man who was doing the best work there was a parson—he happened to be a socialist too. And the reason he had a pull on me was simply that he had the Church behind him. I mean, the whole institution, with its tradition and ritual. You can call it glamour if you like. Anyhow, I learnt its value, and I took orders.'

There was another pause and then Syson wagged his toes again and said, 'I believe Archbishop Temple was a bit shaky about miracles.'

'I shouldn't think many of the bishops take them as a matter of fact, should you?'

'Oh, I see your point—what is the word. You take 'em as religious facts—to give the right feeling.'

'And so they do—as we both know—and to give truth too, the larger truth.'

Syson said nothing to this and Parsloe went on, 'Take the resurrection—its symbolic truth is fundamental—"I am the resurrection and the life." These are good and true words for the individual. And for humanity, isn't it a fact that you can't kill Christ—he rises again for ever.'

Syson had listened to this with his usual rather dreamy expression, stretching out his long legs. He said now, after some moments' reflection, 'I see,' as if agreeing with some general statement about the weather. Then after another pause, he began to draw up his legs as if in preparation for departure.

Parsloe as usual, was slightly exasperated by this curate of his, so energetic when you wanted him to be reserved, so lethargic when you expected him to be interested. He said with emphasis, 'What shall I tell Mantoffle?'

Syson, instead of answering this, said, 'So your position is that miracles are bunk.'

'Good heavens, no. If you think that, you've completely misunderstood.'

'All the same, that would be a clear answer to Preedy.'

'Which unluckily we can't use.'

'No, I suppose not.'

'Do you think he does so much harm?'

'The Church thinks so, though it doesn't seem to care.'

'We're always getting these fellows—revivalists of one kind or another. And I doubt if they do much real harm. More good than harm anyhow. They stir people up—they make 'em realize there's something more in the world than just drawing down your pay and going to the pictures.'

Syson was again silent. He kept silence because he wanted to find some word which would make the man feel what a mean, cowardly creature he was. And yet he knew that this would not be fair, that Parsloe was not a coward or a mean-spirited person. He was doing what he thought to be the wise, the right thing, not only for his people at St. Enoch's but for the Church as a whole.

It was this that so appalled and horrified Syson, the sense of this vast apathy. It was as though the whole organism, the whole immense creature, was lying fat and inert upon the steaming dung-heap of its past slowly dying, already rotting, and in its rottenness poisoning the air for anything young, healthy, that might be trying to draw a first breath of truth.

'I'm sorry,' he said at last. 'But I think I'd better go—I've thought it over for some time.'

This wasn't true. It was an impulse. But now he felt an enormous relief. He was sure that he had done the right thing.

POINTS FOR DISCUSSION

1. 'So your position is that miracles are bunk.' Do you think that this is a fair summing-up of Parsloe's position as far as you can judge from his remarks in this extract?

2. In the introduction, Lord David Cecil refers to people who 'for good or bad reasons feel themselves compelled to accept standards and religious views inherited or imposed on them by society'. Do you think Parsloe falls into this category? If so, do you think any less of him?

(c) *Syson eventually breaks entirely with the Church and loses his faith. He becomes involved with a rationalist group and, continuing his campaign against Preedy, he publishes and distributes a pamphlet containing a criminal libel against him. Arrested for this, he is allowed bail but deliberately persists with his attack and distributes more leaflets while the charge is still in progress against him. He is eventually sentenced to six months' imprisonment. We are told by the author that while in prison he wrote a book called A Sure and Certain Faith and are given this extract from it*

'I hated Preedy, of course. But why? Because those posters of his, those preachings, had shown me that my faith was a muddle of wish-fulfilment and time-serving. He challenged me to state my case and I couldn't do it. I could only fall back on vague statements like "It's all a mystery—the thing is too big for human intelligence." And I knew all the time that if I used arguments like that I'd no right to any reasonable faith at all. You could defend any faith in those terms. Hitlerism, communism. But I believed, or rather I wanted to believe, in a God of love and truth who hated cruelty and injustice, who sought to abolish every kind of evil. Yet here was a man who told me that God could abolish any evil at will, and I was not allowed to believe him. I had to ask the doctors first if God would be any good in this case. That was the ruling of the Church, all the Churches. And I saw at that moment that the Churches did not really believe in this power of God to do miracles. I saw it but dared not admit it. I thought that if I lost my faith in the God that could do miracles I should not believe in him at all—I should lose him altogether and life would not be worth living any more.

'And, in fact, when one day, I realized that I had lost that faith, I did not really want to live any more. I did not want anything from life, neither family happiness, nor even my freedom. I was angry when, that first time, I was saved from jail. I had wished to stay in jail for as long as the courts would keep me there. And that was not because I hated the courts and the law but because I hated life. I longed for the prison which would guard me from life, which would make my existence a mere imitation, a shadow show of life, like that of figures in a clock who do the same things every time the clock strikes, who are simply bits of a machine. I knew, of course, that most people live just such puppet lives, but I had believed that I was free, a free soul serving freely the truth that alone gives freedom.

'But now it seemed to me that I was also a puppet. I was angry with my own vicar because he did not believe with me in the God who could do miracles. I thought him a time-server and a hypo-crite and hated him for a puppet. I thought that the whole world was made of puppets. I believe in the people who say, "There is no freedom—there is no God. We are all simply robots, machines, pushed about by mechanical forces." And I could not bear it. I thought if that is true then I don't want to be made a fool of. If I am a machine let me live the life of a machine.

'So I was angry when they deprived me of jail and I set to work to get back into jail. I don't mean that I said to myself, "I will force them to put me back into jail." I didn't propose any course of action to myself. I had become a puppet pulled about on strings and perhaps it pleased me to give way to the pull of the strings, to behave like a puppet. Perhaps it was because they would not make a puppet of me, in jail, that I wilfully played the puppet out of jail.

'And so I made them send me to jail again. It was my pleasure to be a prisoner because I knew myself a puppet. I saw it was a pleasure but it was the pleasure of the man who hates the whole world, a pleasure like that of a beaten slave who tears open his wounds again and again in revenge upon his slavery.

'But God saved me in the very nick. For I was not taken at once from the court. There was a crowd of people waiting to see me come out and some of these people were very violent against me. So the police planned to take me away by another door, and took me back to a small waiting-room or lodge, and sent for another car in which I could be moved.

'But while we were waiting for this car, a note for me was brought by the constable who was guarding me. He read the note first, explaining that this was now the rule, and then handed it to me.

'It was a letter from a woman, a follower of Preedy, whose child had died. She wrote to say that she had changed her mind about Preedy and wanted to thank me for my efforts to save the child. But she wanted me also to forgive Preedy because he had not meant to do evil. "I know now," she wrote, "that you were right, and God could not save my poor child. But still you were wrong too for he can do miracles. He has done one with me, for he has given me forgiveness and peace. I am all alone in the world now, for my husband has left me, and once I wanted to die. But now I am glad to be alive to remember that happiness when I had my child and to thank God for all the love in the world."

'I remembered this woman very well, and how she had loved her child. And when I read her letter, I was suddenly moved to understand the thing that had stood before my eyes all my life, as wide as the world, as high as the sky, the thing I had repeated a thousand times in prayers and in sermons, without understanding, the miracle of God's love in the world.

'And so I found my truth where I had left it, and I wanted to go out and tell the people. It seemed to me that the truth was so great, so obvious that I had only to speak it and all should know that great joy, all should be free.

'But when I got up and made to leave the lodge, the policeman at the door jumped up and caught my arm and said, "Hullo, where are you off to?" Then I remembered myself and that though I was made free, yet I was a prisoner. This made me laugh, and then the constable at the door of the building called out that they were ready for me. So I went out.'

POINTS FOR DISCUSSION

1. '... if I lost my faith in the God that could do miracles I should not believe in Him at all.' What seems to be the main emphasis in the New Testament—faith as the result of miracles, or miracles as the result of faith? Consider Syson's remark in the light of this.

2. Syson refers to the inadequacy of such statements as, 'It's all a mystery—the thing is too big for human intelligence.' He says that if he used arguments like that he had no right to any reasonable faith at all. Do you agree with him? Do you think that he would have been able to state his case more convincingly after he had discovered that the truth was 'so great, so obvious'?

(d) *The following is an extract from one of Preedy's sermons, preached in the open air. The 'great man' referred to is a well-known journalist*

'A great man, as they think of great men nowadays, a man of power, a man who boasts that he thinks for millions, and blows their minds here and there like gnats on the evening breeze—this great powerful man said to me, "You preachers preach to yourselves. You preach God because you are devils. You preach the life of sacrifice because you need the kick of suffering. You take to Christ as drunkards take to drink, because your batteries are flat, and without juice you're dead."

'And when he said this he thought that he was destroying me— he thought that he was showing me to myself as a worthless person, a fraud, a madman, a self-deceived fool who could not even face the truth about himself.'

These words, shouted in Preedy's big voice, had already caught the ears of bystanders. Passers-by, even city men with rolled umbrellas, had stopped; listeners to other speakers deserted them or stood hovering between Preedy and the next two gatherings. There was already a crowd of thirty or more in front of Preedy and seeing it increase so rapidly, he exulted in his inspiration. He perceived now that God had put that opening into his mouth, and he elaborated it.

'What do you say, friends?' He paused, raised his arms in appeal and bawled aloud. 'What do you think of these words by a great man, a clever man, a teacher and leader of the people—a man with power over millions of homes, millions of parents with children at their knees eager to learn from them the truth of the world. Yes, a man responsible before God for millions of souls. Do you think it is true that Christ is the lord of devils and madmen who fly to him for peace as the lost and forsaken fly to drink and drugs for a moment of forgetfulness?

'Here is a man who hates and fears God, whose religion is money and power, who sacrifices Christ every day of his life, or begs others to do so, do you think he spoke truth when he called the ministers of Christ lunatics, sinners, evil-hearted men, fornicators and adulterers, driven to preach God out of terror and guilt, out of the wickedness of their souls?'

A voice from the back of the crowd shouted 'Yes,' and at once other voices joined in, 'That chap knew something.'

Preedy, as if astonished by these interrupters, threw back his head and hands and stood gazing. Someone at the back laughed.

Preedy let his hands fall. 'Yes, you say yes. And of course you're quite right. That man who spoke to me so, that clever man who said that men fly to God because they are devils, why, of course he was right. For who can save the guilty but Christ, who can purge the filthy mind, the defiled body, but he who is all cleanness, all purity? Who can take away the fear of death, but he who gives life so rich, so proud, that death is but the shadow of its glory?

'I say that clever man, that great man, was right. He was righter even than he knew. It is not only the ministers and preachers of the world who are guilty, who carry in their hearts a fearful emptiness, a fearful question.

'Ask of yourselves. Ask of your own hearts. What do you find there of happiness, of security? You are well today, in good health? At least able to go about the world, to see, to hear, to enjoy food, to work. How long will that last? Till tomorrow? Till tonight? And now you have your jobs, wives and children whom you love. They are waiting for you now. How long will they be

there to wait for you? How long will your happiness last? Do you
think you are sure of your happiness—and what would you do if
you lost it? Would you pity yourselves? Would you curse God?
But why? What right would you have? Did you make this happiness? Did you invent this love? What have you done to deserve it,
to deserve your health, your pay, your loves? What have you
given for them? What have you done to earn them? Look in your
souls and ask. Would you dare tell any man what you find there?
Would you dare whisper it even to those who love you, to whisper
it even in the dark—those secret thoughts, those secret desires, the
cowardice and the lies, the tricks and the meanness, the selfishness
and the greed? Would you even admit them to yourselves? Would
you dare to tell the truth in your own mind? Would you not
rather find the speck in your brother's eye than the cataract in
your own? Of course you would. Everybody would. And that is
why that man of power, that great and clever man was so eager to
prove to me that the ministers of God are really men of the devil,
men so wicked that they need God and cling to him as drowning
men cling to a raft.

'He was right, why should he not be right? He is a clever man.
He has read all the books, he has studied logic. He can prove anything, he can make words do his every will. For him, they fly like
birds, they dance like girls, they sing like angels, they wound like
guns, they cure like the wisest doctors, they kill like the subtlest
poison, sinking day by day into the secret places of the soul, creeping through vein and nerve, till a man is changed into a drivelling
beast, a raving maniac.

'But see, the words take their revenge. The great man, the clever
man, has swallowed his own poison. He has said to himself, "All
men are sinners except myself—all men deceive themselves except
me. I am too clever." '

The sky clouded over, swiftly, darkly. 'My brothers, men are
prisoners of darkness in cells expecting execution—condemned
cells. They interpret the world by its noises—jail noises—and
react in their various ways, resigned, frightened, angry, sullen,
defiant, or full of some crazy hope of escape, a reprieve, a revolution, a thunderbolt to split the wall, the end of the world or the
beginning of the millenium.

'To each of them the world is simply a condemned cell where
he is locked up alone. He knows his fellow prisoners only as distant
and mysterious cries. All the affairs of the world come to him as

the disconnected noises of a jail, incomprehensible, terrifying. He is lucky if he can distract himself with books or catching flies, call himself a philosopher for being callous and resigned, shut his ears to the screams from the torture chambers with their ingenious machinery for breaking bones and nerve. But most hear little else and carry on as best they can, because they must—some with bluster and defiance, some with——'

The inky cloud had blown over and suddenly the sun broke through. Preedy abruptly abandoned his argument and changed his tone and gestures. 'But God sends his light upon the world.' He raised his face to the sky and threw up his right hand, 'Like the sun that pierces the very earth. See the trees are standing bare and as if dead. To themselves they are dead. But the sun will not allow them to die. He sends his light to their roots, and there, unknown to the bare branches, the sap is rising, the life they deny is rising through their cells.

'So life rises in the souls of men, whether they would or not. And so the light of grace drives the sap through dead words and brings them to life, to a new harvest of beauty and at last the seed. So some men by grace realize their living power and their death. But the clever men refuse the light because they are afraid—they live in a tent of words, they weave over their heads a roof of logic, with strong beams of science, and tiles of self-sufficiency, corrugated glass and concrete spite, so that they can live in the warm dark with the rats and the bugs.

'Why then did that great man, that powerful man come to me and say, "I know you—you are one who believes in God because of your need?" Because he himself was afraid, because he himself was in need. Because he was terrified of the light that would show him his mean little soul, the need that would make him cry out for forgiveness.'

POINTS FOR DISCUSSION

1. Consider Preedy's sermon. Cary clearly thinks that Preedy's religion is more the 'real thing' than was Syson's before his conversion. Why do you think this is so?

2. On what grounds could you criticize Preedy's sermon for being merely 'street-corner oratory'? Is it anything more than this?

12. HENRIK IBSEN

BRAND

HENRIK IBSEN was born at Skien in Norway in 1828. When he was fifteen his father's business suffered a financial disaster and he was apprenticed to an apothecary at Grimstad, a tiny seaport further down the coast, and there he spent six years in poverty and isolation. He was interested in poetry and drama at an early age, and wrote his first play, *Catiline*, as early as 1849. After a rather unsuccessful spell as a student at the university in Christiania (Oslo), he became, in 1851, the stage-manager at the newly-formed National Theatre in Bergen, and remained there for six years, writing and directing plays. He continued, however, to be plagued by poverty and despair, and did not achieve any real success until the production in 1864 of his play *The Pretenders* at the Christiania Theatre, to which he had just been appointed as literary adviser. In the same year he left for Rome, and for the next twenty-seven years he lived abroad, mainly in Rome, Dresden, and Munich. It was in Rome that he wrote *Brand*, a verse play for reading and not intended for production on the stage. It was published in 1866 and was an immediate and immense success, and brought him fame throughout Scandinavia. *Peer Gynt* followed in 1867, and *Emperor and Galilean* in 1873. Between 1875 and the end of the century he wrote the twelve great prose dramas (including *A Doll's House, Ghosts, The Wild Duck,* and *Hedda Gabler*) which earned him his international reputation as one of the greatest European dramatists. He returned to live in Norway in 1891 and died there in 1906.

In a letter written in 1880 Ibsen wrote:

> Everything that I have written has the closest possible connection with what I have lived through ... in every new poem or play I have aimed at my own spiritual emancipation and purification— for a man shares the responsibility and the guilt of the society to which he belongs.

Thus Ibsen often seems to be conducting an intense inner dialogue with himself in his plays, which show deep psychological insight and deal with the great problems and discords of human nature and human society, and in particular with the theme of vocation, the quest of the individual for self-realization.

Brand, from which the following extract is taken, is set in and around a village on the west coast of Norway, and in the mountains above it; the time is the middle of the nineteenth century. It is the story of the quest for truth and self-realization of Brand, a priest who is deeply contemptuous of the half-hearted beliefs of contemporary Christians. He is possessed by a militant and fanatical urge to regenerate humanity and to recall men to a religion which embraces the whole of life; his slogan is 'All or Nothing'. He feels that the call of God demands everything of him, and he demands that others also shall sacrifice everything which God demands. If such sacrifice brings unhappiness, it is of no importance compared with the betrayal involved in refusing to follow the absolute demands which all men experience in the depths of their hearts. Brand's single-mindedness stands in impressive contrast to the everyday half-measures and compromises, and emphasizes the necessity of following one's private conscience and 'being oneself'. But the play does not shirk the intolerance which results from such uncompromising commitment, and the question of how much should be sacrificed to the demands of a burning mission or vocation remains unanswered. Brand's attitude is criticized during the play by one of the characters as follows:

> You still want to resurrect an age that is dead.
> You still preach the pact that Jehovah
> Made with man five thousand years ago.
> Every generation must make its own pact with God.
> Our generation is not to be scared by rods
> Of fire, or by nurses' tales about damned souls.
> Its first commandment, Brand, is: Be humane.

Brand's reply is:

> Humane! That word excuses all our weakness.
> Was God humane towards Jesus Christ?

The following extract starts at the opening of the play.

In the snow, high up in the wilds of the mountains. Mist hangs densely. It is raining, and nearly dark. BRAND, *dressed in black, with pack and staff, is struggling towards the west. His companions, a* GUIDE *and the* GUIDE'S YOUNG SON, *follow a short distance behind.*

GUIDE [*shouts after* BRAND]:
  Hi, there, stranger! Don't go so fast!
  Where are you?

BRAND: Here.
GUIDE: You'll lose your way. This mist's so thick
  I can hardly see the length of my staff.
SON: Father, there's a crack in the snow!
GUIDE: A crevasse!
BRAND: We have lost all trace of the path.
GUIDE [*shouts*]: Stop, man, for God's sake. The glacier's
  As thin as a crust here. Tread lightly.
BRAND [*listening*]: I can hear the roar of a waterfall.
GUIDE: A river has hollowed its way beneath us.
  There's an abyss here too deep to fathom.
  It will swallow us up.
BRAND: I must go on. I told you before.
GUIDE: It's beyond mortal power. Feel!
  The ground here is hollow and brittle.
  Stop! It's life or death.
BRAND: I must. I serve a great master.
GUIDE: What's his name?
BRAND: His name is God.
GUIDE: Who are you?
BRAND: A priest.
GUIDE [*goes cautiously closer*]:
  Listen, priest. We've only one life.
  Once that's lost, we don't get another.
  There's a frozen mountain lake ahead,
  And mountain lakes are treacherous.
BRAND: We will walk across it.
GUIDE: Walk on water? [*Laughs.*]
BRAND: It has been done.
GUIDE: Ah, that was long ago. There are no miracles now.
  You sink without trace.
BRAND: Farewell. [*Begins to move on.*]
GUIDE: You'll die.
BRAND: If my master needs my death
    Then welcome flood and cataract and storm.
GUIDE [*quietly*]: He's mad.
SON [*almost crying*]:
  Father, let's turn back. There's a storm coming on.
BRAND [*stops, and goes back towards them*]: Listen, guide.
  Didn't you say your daughter has sent you word
  That she is dying, and cannot go in peace

Unless she sees you first?

GUIDE: It's true, God help me.

BRAND: And she cannot live beyond today?

GUIDE: Yes.

BRAND: Then, come!

GUIDE: It's impossible. Turn back.

BRAND [*gazes at him*]:

What would you give for your daughter to die in peace?

GUIDE: I'd give everything I have, my house and farm, gladly.

BRAND: But not your life?

GUIDE: My life?

BRAND: Well?

GUIDE: There's a limit. I've a wife and children at home.

BRAND: Go home. Your life is the way of death.

You do not know God, and God does not know you.

GUIDE: You're hard.

SON [*tugging at his coat*]: Come on, father.

GUIDE: All right. But he must come too.

BRAND: Must I? [*Turns. A hollow roar is heard in the distance.*]

SON [*screams*]: An avalanche!

BRAND [*to the* GUIDE, *who has grabbed him by the collar*]: Let go!

GUIDE: No.

BRAND: Let go at once!

GUIDE [*wrestling with* BRAND]: No, the Devil take me——'

BRAND [*tears himself loose, and throws the* GUIDE *in the snow*]:

He will, you can be sure. In the end.

GUIDE [*sits rubbing his arm*]:

Ah! Stubborn fool! But he's strong.

So that's what he calls the Lord's work.

[*Shouts, as he gets up.*] Hi, priest!

SON: He's gone over the pass.

GUIDE: I can still see him. [*Shouts again.*] Hi, there!

Where did we leave the road?

BRAND [*from the mist*]:

You need no signpost. Your road is broad enough.

GUIDE: I wish to God it was.

Then I'd be warm at home by nightfall.

He and his SON *exeunt towards the east.*

BRAND [*appears higher up, and looks in the direction in which they have gone*]:

They grope their way home. You coward!
If you'd had the will and only lacked the strength,
I would have helped you. Footsore as I am,
I could have carried you on my tired back
Gladly and easily. [*Moves on again.*]
Ha; how men love life! They'll sacrifice
Anything else, but life—no, that must be saved.
   He smiles, as though remembering something.
When I was a boy, I remember,
Two thoughts kept occurring to me, and made me laugh.
An owl frightened by darkness, and a fish
Afraid of water. Why did I think of them?
Because I felt, dimly, the difference
Between what is and what should be; between
Having to endure, and finding one's burden
Unendurable.
            Every man
Is such an owl and such a fish, created
To work in darkness, to live in the deep;
And yet he is afraid. He splashes
In anguish towards the shore, stares at the bright
Vault of heaven, and screams: 'Give me air
And the blaze of day.'
What was that? It sounded like singing.
Yes, there it is—laughter and song.
The sun shines. The mist is lifting.
Now I see the whole mountain plain.
A happy crowd of people stands
In the morning sunshine on the mountain top.
Now they are separating. The others
Turn to the east, but two go westwards.
They wave farewell.
   *The sun breaks more brightly through the mist. He stands
   looking down at the approaching figures.*
            Light shines about these two
It is as though the mist fell back before them,
As though heather clothed every slope and ridge
And the sky smiled on them. They must be
Brother and sister. Hand in hand they run
Over the carpet of heather.
   EJNAR *and* AGNES, *warm and glowing, in light travelling*

*clothes, come dancing along the edge of the crevasse. The mist
has dispersed, and a clear summer morning lies over the
.mountain.*

EJNAR [*sings*]: Agnes, my butterfly,
   You know I will capture you yet.
   Though you fly, it will not save you,
   For soon you'll be caught in my net.
AGNES [*sings, dancing backwards in front of him, evading him
            continuously*]: If I am your butterfly,
   With joy and delight I shall play,
   But if you should catch me,
   Don't crush my wings, I pray.
EJNAR: On my hand I shall lift you,
   In my heart I shall lock you away,
   And for ever, my butterfly,
   Your joyful game you can play.
      Without noticing it, EJNAR *and* AGNES *have come to the edge
      of the crevasse, and now stand on the brink.*
BRAND [*calling down to them*]:
   Stop! You're on the edge of a precipice!
EJNAR: Who's that shouting?
AGNES [*points upwards*]: Look!
BRAND: That snowdrift's hollow.
   It's hanging over the edge of the precipice.
   Save yourselves before it's too late!
EJNAR [*throws his arms round her and laughs up at him*]:
   We're not afraid.
AGNES: We haven't finished.
   Our game; we've a whole lifetime yet.
EJNAR: We've been given a hundred years.
   Together in the sun.
BRAND: And then?
EJNAR: Then? Home again. [*Points to the sky.*] To Heaven.
BRAND: Ah! That's where you've come from, is it?
EJNAR: Of course. Where else? Come down here,
   And I'll tell you how good God has been to us.
   Then you'll understand the power of joy.
   Don't stand up there like an icicle. Come on down!
   Good! First, I'm a painter,
   And it's a wonderful thing to give my thoughts flight,
   Charming dead colours into life

As God creates a butterfly out of a chrysalis.
But the most wonderful thing God ever did
Was to give me Agnes for my bride.
I was coming from the south, after a long
Journey, with my easel on my back——
AGNES [*eagerly*]: As bold as a king, fresh and gay,
Knowing a thousand songs.
EJNAR: As I was coming through the pass, I saw her.
She had come to drink the mountain air,
The sunshine, the dew, and the scent of the pines.
Some force had driven me up to the mountains.
A voice inside me said:
'Seek beauty where the pine trees grow,
By the forest river, high among the clouds.'
There I painted my masterpiece,
A blush on her cheek, two eyes bright with happiness,
A smile that sang from her heart.
I asked her to marry me, and she said yes.
They gave a feast for us which lasted three days.
Everyone was there. We tried to slip away
Last night, but they followed us, waving flags,
Leaves in their hats, singing all the way.
The mist was heavy from the north,
But it fell back before us.
BRAND: Where are you going now?
EJNAR: Over that last mountain peak, westwards down
To the mouth of the fjord, and then home to the city
For our wedding feast as fast as ship can sail
Then south together, like swans on their first flight——
BRAND: And there?
EJNAR: A happy life
Together, like a dream, like a fairy tale.
For this Sunday morning, out there on the mountain,
Without a priest, our lives were declared free
Of sorrow, and consecrated to happiness.
BRAND: By whom?
EJNAR: By everyone.
BRAND: Farewell. [*Turns to go.*]
EJNAR [*suddenly looks closely at him in surprise*]:
No, wait. Don't I know your face?
BRAND [*coldly*]: I am a stranger.

EJNAR: I'm sure I remember——
  Could we have known each other at school—or at home?
BRAND: Yes, we were friends at school. But then
  I was a boy. Now I am a man.
EJNAR: It can't be——[*Shouts suddenly.*] Brand! Yes, it's you!
BRAND: I knew you at once.
EJNAR: How good to see you!
  Look at me! Yes, you're the same old Brand,
  Who always kept to yourself and never played
  With us.
BRAND: No, I was not at home.
  Among you southerners. I was
  Of another race, born by a cold fjord,
  In the shadow of a barren mountain.
EJNAR: Is your home in these parts?
BRAND: My road will take me through it.
EJNAR: Through it? You're going beyond, then?
BRAND: Yes, beyond; far beyond my home.
EJNAR: Are you a priest now?
BRAND: A mission preacher. I live
  One day in one place, the next in another.
EJNAR: Where are you bound?
BRAND [*sharply*]: Don't ask that.
EJNAR: Why?
BRAND [*changes his tone*]:
  Well, the ship which is waiting for you will take me too.
EJNAR: Agnes, he's coming the same way!
BRAND: Yes; but I am going to a burial feast.
AGNES: To a burial feast?
EJNAR: Who is to be buried?
BRAND: That God you have just called yours.
AGNES: Come, Ejnar.
EJNAR: Brand!
BRAND: The God of every dull and earthbound slave
  Shall be shrouded and coffined for all to see
  And lowered into his grave. It is time, you know.
  He has been ailing for a thousand years.
EJNAR: Brand, you're ill!
BRAND: No, I am well and strong
  As mountain pine or juniper. It is
  Our time, our generation, that is sick

And must be cured. All you want is to flirt,
And play, and laugh; to do lip-service to your faith
But not to know the truth; to leave your suffering
To someone who they say died for your sake.
He died for you, so you are free to dance.
To dance, yes; but whither?
Ah, that is another thing, my friend.

EJNAR: Oh, I see. This is the new teaching.
You're one of those pulpit-thumpers who tell us
That all joy is vanity, and hope
The fear of hell will drive us into sackcloth.

BRAND: No. I do not speak for the Church. I hardly
Know if I'm a Christian. But I know
That I am a man. And I know what it is
That has drained away our spirit.

EJNAR [smiles]: We usually have the reputation of being
Too full of spirit.

BRAND: You don't understand me.
It isn't love of pleasure that is destroying us.
It would be better if it were.
Enjoy life if you will,
But be consistent, do it all the time,
Not one thing one day and another the next.
Be wholly what you are, not half and half.
Everyone now is a little of everything;
A little solemn on Sundays, a little respectful
Towards tradition; makes love to his wife after Saturday
Supper, because his father did the same.
A little gay at feasts, a little lavish
In giving promises, but niggardly
In fulfilling them; a little of everything;
A little sin, a little virtue;
A little good, a little evil; the one
Destroys the other, and every man is nothing.

EJNAR: All right. I agree that we are sinful.
But what has that to do with Him
You want to bury—the God I still call mine?

BRAND: My gay friend, show me this God of yours.
You're an artist. You've painted him, I hear.
He's old, isn't he?

EJNAR: Well—yes.

BRAND: Of course.
  And grey, and thin on top, as old men are?
  Kindly, but severe enough to frighten
  Children into bed? Did you give him slippers?
  I hope you allowed him spectacles and a skull-cap.
EJNAR [*angrily*]: What do you mean.
BRAND: That's just what he is,
  The God of our country, the people's God.
  A feeble dotard in his second childhood.
  You would reduce God's kingdom,
  A kingdom which should stretch from pole to pole,
  To the confines of the Church. You separate
  Life from faith and doctrine. You do not want
  To live your faith. For that you need a God
  Who'll keep one eye shut. That God is getting feeble
  Like the generation that worships him.
  Mine is a storm where yours is a gentle wind,
  Inflexible where yours is deaf, all-loving,
  Not all-doting. And He is young
  And strong like Hercules. His is the voice
  That spoke in thunder when He stood
  Bright before Moses in the burning bush,
  A giant before the dwarf of dwarfs. In the valley
  Of Gideon He stayed the sun, and worked
  Miracles without number—and would work
  Them still, if people were not dead, like you.
EJNAR [*smiles uncertainly*]: And now we are to be created anew?
BRAND: Yes. As surely as I know that I
  Was born into this world to heal its sickness
  And its weakness.
EJNAR: Do not blow out the match because it smokes
  Before the lantern lights the road.
  Do not destroy the old language
  Until you have created the new.
BRAND: I do not seek
  To create anything new. I uphold
  What is eternal. I do not come
  To bolster dogmas or the Church.
  They were born and they will die.
  But one thing cannot die; the Spirit, not created, but
    eternal,

Redeemed by Christ when it had been forfeited
In the first fresh spring of time. He threw a bridge
Of human faith from flesh back to the Spirit's source.
Now it is hawked round piecemeal, but from these stumps
Of soul, from these severed heads and hands,
A whole shall rise which God shall recognize,
Man, His greatest creation, His chosen heir,
Adam, young and strong.

EJNAR [*interrupts*]: Goodbye. I think we had better part.

BRAND: Go westwards. I go to the north. There are two
Roads to the fjord. One is as short as the other.
Farewell.

EJNAR: Goodbye.

BRAND [*turns as he is about to descend*]:
There is darkness and there is light. Remember,
Living is an art.

EJNAR [*waving him away*]: Turn the world upside down.
I still have faith in my God.

BRAND: Good; but paint him
With crutches. I go to lay him in his grave.
He goes down the path. EJNAR *goes silently and looks after
him.*

AGNES [*stands for a moment as though abstracted; then starts and
looks round uneasily*]: Has the sun gone down?

EJNAR: No, it was only
A cloud passing. Soon it will shine again.

AGNES: There's a cold wind.

EJNAR: It was a gust
Blowing through the gap. Let's go down.

AGNES: How black the mountain has become, shutting
Our road to the south.

EJNAR: You were so busy singing
And playing, you didn't notice it until
He frightened you with his shouting. Let him follow
His narrow path. We can go on with our game.

POINTS FOR DISCUSSION

1. What does Brand object to in the religious attitude of the guide?

2. Discuss the meaning of Brand's story of the owl and the fish. What connection do you think it has (*a*) with Brand's conversation with the guide and (*b*) with the idea of lives 'consecrated to happiness' mentioned by Ejnar later on?

3. Compare Brand's idea of God with that of Ejnar.

4. To what extent is Ejnar's religious attitude still recognizable among Christians today?

5. Do you agree with the comments of the character quoted in the introduction to this extract?

6. Discuss Brand's reply to the remarks of this character.

7. What parts of the New Testament would you look to for help in solving the problems posed by Brand's slogan of 'All or Nothing'?

13. JOHN WHITING

THE DEVILS

JOHN WHITING (1915–1963) took the theme of *The Devils* from a book by Aldous Huxley called *The Devils of Loudun*. In this book Huxley describes a strange series of events which are recorded as having taken place in the French town of Loudun between the years 1623 and 1634. A convent of nuns was supposed to be in the grip of possession by devils; the communal hysteria which broke out arose from an obsession which the Prioress of the convent (Sister Jeanne) had for Urbain Grandier, the vicar of St. Peter's Church, who is the central character of Whiting's play. Grandier is a highly complex and paradoxical character in whom an unscrupulous sexuality and a considerable self-conceit battle against a very real and profound desire to find God. Grandier has long been in the habit of reserving his Tuesday afternoons for visits to the complaisant widows of Loudun, and early on in the play we see him praying:

> O my dear Father, it is the wish of Your humble child to come to your Grace. I speak in the weariness of thirty-five years. Years heavy with pride and ambition, love of women and love of self. Years scandalously marred by adornment and luxury, time taken up with being that nothing, a man.
>
> I prostrate myself before You now in ravaged humility of spirit. I ask You to look upon me with love. I beg that You will answer my prayer. Show me a way. Or let a way be made. [*Silence*]
>
> O God, O my God, my God! Release me! Free me! These needs! Have mercy. Free me. Four o'clock of a Tuesday afternoon. Free me. [*He rises: cries out*] Rex tremendae majestatis, qui salvandos salvas gratis, salva me, fons pietatis!

Eventually he turns away from these practices with loathing and satiety, but not before his powerful physical attractions have aroused the Prioress and some of her nuns to such a wild and hysterical pitch of jealousy that they are believed to be possessed by devils through the agency of Grandier and his alliance with them. As a result, Grandier is arrested and imprisoned; he is humiliated and tortured (both his legs are shattered below the knee) and finally burnt at the stake, refusing all chances of confessing to the sorcery he is accused of. Thus he finds in his martyrdom the God he has so long been searching for; as his shattered body is carried to the stake, his final words are, 'Look at this thing which I am, and learn the meaning of love.'

The first extract below is an account by Grandier of a profound experience he had of God after he had put a stop to his sexual encounters and just before his arrest. The second extract takes place in Grandier's cell immediately before he is led out to his trial and torture.

In her book *With Love to the Church*, Monica Furlong says of this passage:

> In his talk of creating God, Whiting cuts across orthodox theology in a single Promethean stroke that acknowledges our humanism, our post-Freudian knowledge of ourselves. When he goes on to speak of the presence, the giving, the summons to adoration and worship, he acknowledges the Other of which theology has spoken continually.

This passage is of particular interest today when many theologians such as Paul Tillich (in *The Shaking of the Foundations*) and the former Bishop of Woolwich (in *Honest to God*) are urging people to look for God, the immanent God, in their own selves, in their relationships and in the 'depth of their being'. The following passage from a sermon by Tillich is an example:

> The wisdom of all ages and of all continents speaks about the road to our depth. It has been described in innumerable different ways. But all those who have been concerned—mystics and priests, poets and philosophers, simple people and educated people—with that road through confession, lonely self-scrutiny, internal or external catastrophes, prayer, contemplation, have witnessed to the same experience. They have found that they were not what they believed themselves to be, even after a deeper level had appeared to them below the vanishing surface.... Today a new form of this method has become famous, the so-called 'psychology of depth'. It leads us from the surface of our self-knowledge into levels where things are recorded which we knew nothing about on the surface of our consciousness.... It can help us to find the way into our depth, although it cannot help us in an ultimate way, because it cannot guide us to the deepest ground of our being and of all being, the depth of life itself. The name of this infinite and inexhaustible depth and ground of all being is *God*. The depth is what the word *God* means. And if that word has not much meaning for you, translate it, and speak of the depths of your life, of the source of your being, of your ultimate concern, of what you take seriously without any reservation. Perhaps in order to do so you must forget everything traditional that you have learned about God, perhaps even that word itself. For if you know that God means depth, you know much about

Him. You cannot then call yourself an atheist or unbeliever. For you cannot think or say: Life has no depth! Life itself is shallow. Being itself is surface only. If you could say this in complete seriousness, you would be an atheist; but otherwise you are not. He who knows about depth, knows about God.

Both the following extracts should be read before attempting the points for discussion.

(a) *Just before his arrest, Grandier has a profound experience of God*

A brilliant morning.

[GRANDIER *comes to the Sewerman, carrying flowers.*]

SEWERMAN: Why, whatever's this?

GRANDIER: I must have picked them somewhere. I can't remember. You have them.

SEWERMAN: Thank you. They smell sweet. Very suitable.

GRANDIER: Can I sit with you?

SEWERMAN: Of course. I've no sins this morning though. Sorry.

GRANDIER: Let me look at you.

SEWERMAN: Do you like what you see?

GRANDIER: Very much.

SEWERMAN: What's happened? You're drunk with mystery.

GRANDIER: I've been out of the town. An old man was dying. I sat with him for two nights and a day. I was seeing death for the hundredth time. It was an obscene struggle. It always is. Once again a senile, foolish, and sinful old man had left it rather late to come to terms. He held my hand so tightly that I could not move. His grimy face stared up at me in blank surprise at what was happening to him. So I sat there in the rancid smell of the kitchen, while in the darkness the family argued in whispers, between weeping, about how much money there would be under the bed.

He was dirty and old and not very bright. And I loved him so much. I envied him so much, for he was standing on the threshold of everlasting life. I wanted him to turn his face to God, and not peer back through the smoky light, and stare longingly at this mere preliminary. I said to him: Be glad, be glad. But he did not understand.

His spirit weakened at dawn. It could not mount another day. There were cries of alarm from the family. I took out the necessary properties which I travel in this bag. The vulgar little sins were confessed, absolved, and the man could die. He did so. Brutally, holding on to the last. I spoke my usual words to the family, with my priest's face. My duty was done.

But I could not forget my love for the man.

I came out of the house. I thought I'd walk back, air myself after the death cell. I was very tired. I could hear Saint Peter's bell.

The road was dusty. I remembered the day I came here. I was wearing new shoes. They were white with dust. Do you know, I flicked them over with my stole before being received by the bishop. I was vain and foolish, then. Ambitious, too.

I walked on. They were working in the fields and called to me. I remembered how I loved to work with my hands when I was a boy. But my father said it was unsuitable for one of my birth.

I could see my church in the distance. I was very proud, in a humble way. I thought of my love for the beauty of this not very beautiful place. And I remembered night in the building, with the gold, lit by candlelight, against the darkness.

I thought of you. I remembered you as a friend.

I rested. The country was stretched out. Do you know where the rivers join? I once made love there.

Children came past me. Yes, of course, that's where I got the flowers. I didn't pick them. They were given to me.

I watched the children go. Yes, I was very tired. I could see far beyond the point my eyes could see. Castles, cities, mountains, oceans, plains, forests—and——

And then—oh, my son, my son—and then—I want to tell you——

SEWERMAN: Do so. Be calm.

GRANDIER: My son, I—Am I mad?

SEWERMAN: No. Quite sane. Tell me, What did you do?

GRANDIER: I created God!

[*Silence.*]

GRANDIER: I created Him from the light and the air, from the dust of the road, from the sweat of my hands, from gold, from filth, from the memory of women's faces, from great rivers, from children, from the works of man, from the past, the present, the future, and the unknown. I caused Him to be from fear and despair. I gathered in everything from this mighty act, all I have known, seen, and experimented. My sin, my presumption, my vanity, my love, my hate, my lust. And last I gave myself and so made God. And He was magnificent. For He is all these things.

I was utterly in his presence. I knelt by the road. I took out the bread and the wine. Panem vinum in salutis consecramus hostiam. And in this understanding He gave Himself humbly and faithfully to me, as I had given myself to Him.

[*Silence.*]

SEWERMAN: You've found peace.

GRANDIER: More. I've found meaning.

SEWERMAN: That makes me happy.

GRANDIER: And, my son, I have found reason.

SEWERMAN: And that is sanity.

GRANDIER: I must go now. I must go to worship Him in His house, adore Him in His shrine. I must go to church.

[GRANDIER *moves forward and enters the church.*]

(b) Grandier awaits torture and his final martyrdom

[GRANDIER *alone in his cell.*]

GRANDIER: There will be pain. It will kill God. My fear is driving Him out already.

Yes. Yes. We are flies upon the wall. Buzzing in the heat. That's so. That's so. No, no. We're monsters made up in a day. Clay in a baby's hands. Horrible, we should be bottled and hung in the pharmacy. Curiosities, for amusement only.

So. Nothing.

Shall I withstand the pain? Mother, mother, remember my fear! Oh, nothing. This morning on the road. What was that? It was a little delusion of meaning. A trick of the sun, some fatigue of the body, and a man starts to believe that he's immortal. Look at me now. Wringing my hands, trying to convince myself that this flesh and bone is meaningful.

Sad, sad, though, very sad. To make a man see in the morning what the glory might be, and by night to snatch it from him.

Most Heavenly Father, though I struggle in Your arms like a fretful child——

This need to create a meaning. What arrogance it is! Expendable, that's what we are. Nothing proceeding to nothing.

Let me look into this void. Let me look into myself. Is there one thing, past or present, which makes for a purpose? [*Silence.*] Nothing. Nothing.

Who's there?

[FATHER AMBROSE, *an old man, has come in.*]

AMBROSE: My name is Ambrose.

GRANDIER: I know you, Father.

AMBROSE: I was told of your trouble, my son. The night can be very long.

GRANDIER: Yes. Stay with me.

AMBROSE: I thought I might read to you. Or, if you'd like it better, we can pray together.

GRANDIER: No. Help me.

AMBROSE: Let me try.

GRANDIER: They are destroying my faith. By fear and loneliness now. Later by pain.

AMBROSE: Go to God, my son.

GRANDIER: Nothing going to nothing.

AMBROSE: God is here, and Christ is now.

GRANDIER: Yes. That is my faith. But how can I defend it?

AMBROSE: By remembering the will of God.

GRANDIER: Yes. Yes.

AMBROSE: By remembering that nothing must be asked of him, and nothing refused.

GRANDIER: Yes. But this is all in the books. I've read them, and understood them. And it is not enough. Not enough. Not now.

AMBROSE: God is here, and Christ is here.

GRANDIER: You're an old man. Have you gathered no more than this fustian in all your years? I'm sorry. You came in pure charity. The only one who has done so. I'm sorry.

[AMBROSE *opens a book.*]

AMBROSE: Suffering must be willed, affliction must be willed, humiliation must be willed, and in the act of willing——

GRANDIER: They'll be understood. I know. I know.

AMBROSE: Then you know everything.

GRANDIER: I know nothing. Speak to me as a man, Father. Talk about simple things.

AMBROSE: I came to help you, my son.

GRANDIER: You can help me. By speaking as a man. So shut your books. Forget other men's words. Speak to me.

AMBROSE: Ah, you believe there is some secret in simplicity. I am a simple man, it's true. I've never had any great doubt. Plain and shy, I have been less tempted than others, of course. The devil likes more magnificence than I've ever been able to offer. A peasant boy who clung to the love of God because he was too awkward to ask for the love of man. I'm not a good example, my son. That's why I brought the books.

GRANDIER: You think too little of yourself. What must we give God?

AMBROSE: Ourselves.

GRANDIER: But I am unworthy.

AMBROSE: Have you greatly sinned?

GRANDIER: Greatly.

AMBROSE: Even young girls come to me nowadays and confess things I don't know about. So it's hardly likely that I'll understand the sins of a young man of the world such as you. But let me try.

GRANDIER: There have been women and lust: power and ambition: worldliness and mockery.

AMBROSE: Remember. God is here. You speak before Him. Christ is now. You suffer with Him.

GRANDIER: I dread the pain to come. The humiliation.

AMBROSE: Did you dread the ecstasy of love?

GRANDIER: No.

AMBROSE: Or its humiliation?

GRANDIER: I gloried in it. I have lived by the senses.

AMBROSE: Then die by them.

GRANDIER: What did you say?

AMBROSE: Offer God pain, convulsion, and disgust.

GRANDIER: Yes. Give Him myself.

AMBROSE: Let Him reveal Himself in the only way you can understand.

GRANDIER: Yes! Yes!

AMBROSE: It is all any of us can do. We live a little while, and in that little while we sin. We go to Him as we can. All is forgiven.

GRANDIER: Yes. I am His child. It is true. Let Him take me as I am. So there is meaning. There is meaning, after all. I am a sinful man and I can be accepted. It is not nothing going to nothing. It is sin going to forgiveness. It is a human creature going to love.

POINTS FOR DISCUSSION

1. 'I created God.' Is this an outrageous blasphemy? Or is it a statement meaningless as it stands, but which could be made acceptable by the substitution of another word for 'created'? Or does it express, poetically if you like, some aspect of the truth about God's relationship with his creation?

2. Note how Grandier later describes his experience. 'It was a little delusion of meaning. A trick of the sun, some fatigue of the body and a man starts to believe that he's immortal.' Consider what parts these sudden moments of illumination or intuition have played in the lives of great men, whether religious or not. Are we right to be as sceptical of them as Grandier appears here?

3. Consider the following comment on the passage from Tillich '... the conversion of the unbeliever is only so easy for Tillich because belief in God has been evacuated of all its traditional content. It now consists in moral seriousness and nothing more.'[1] Do you think that Tillich is using religious language to cloak what is in fact atheism?

4. How is it that Father Ambrose is able to persuade Grandier that he is not 'nothing going to nothing'? At what point do you think that Grandier begins to feel that what the old man has to say is not mere 'fustian'?

[1] Alasdair MacIntyre, 'God and the Theologians', *Encounter*, September 1963.

14. PETRU DUMITRIU

INCOGNITO

PETRU DUMITRIU was born in Rumania in 1924. He started writing
novels at an early age and quickly established a reputation. He became
the Director of the State Publishing House, but eventually found that
he could no longer accept the practices of the Communist regime and
in 1960, while travelling abroad on a cultural mission, he managed to
escape to the West by way of East Berlin. He now lives in Frankfurt.
Dumitriu's novels are not well known in this country, although *Incognito*, from which these extracts come, is the third of his books to have
been published here. It was first published in 1962, the English translation appearing in 1964.

The story of *Incognito* is set in Rumania and is mainly concerned
with the life of Sebastian Ionesco, who is the narrator in all the extracts below. As a young man, Sebastian had been converted to Communism; he had taken part in the fighting against the Nazis, and in the
post-war period he was making a promising career in the security
police. But he becomes disgusted with the methods used by the regime
he represents and he resigns his post. He is expelled from the Party and
is eventually imprisoned. It is in the filth and degradation of the
prison that he discovers the faith for which he has been searching so
long—a faith in the God who dwells *incognito* in everything.

(a) *Sebastian's moment of conversion in prison*

When the guard came in with my can of soup I was seated on my
bed, stiff with hatred. He thrust the can at me. I said:

'Clear out!'

He put it down beside me on the bare planks of the bed, and I
shouted at him:

'Take it away!'

He jumped back as though he had been hit in the stomach. He
could see my face, but I did not see his until he was outside the
cell and in the act of closing the door—it was white. He slammed
the door and slid the bolt. A few minutes later four men appeared.

He had been so afraid I was going to kill him with my bare hands
—and indeed I had been near to doing it—that he had raised the
alarm. They picked me up by the arms and legs, carted me along
those endless concrete corridors to an open trap door, dropped me
in and closed it. While they were carrying me I told myself that
this must be brought to an end. I would smash my head against the
wall the first chance I got. Or else I would go mad, like Bulz—I
knew now that anyone can go mad, if they want to enough. Suicide
and madness were still open to me as ways of escape. I was at the
top of the slope, but it was a very slippery one; I had only to let
myself go.

With hands and knees bruised by the fall, my whole body that
of a sick man, I stayed motionless for a moment, thinking—'Now!'
But there was no hurry, I could take my time. I needed, in any
case, to find out how far away the wall was. I groped with hands and
feet. I was in a hole the shape of a cube, damp and empty and
smelling strongly of excrement—I found the filth-encrusted hole
in the concrete floor which served as a latrine. A new, strange feeling came over me, a near-gaiety and near-serenity. Everything
was simple. I could escape whenever I chose from the monstrous
evil that afflicted me. I was innocent, I was being made to suffer for
no reason, I would escape from my torment, it was simple.

'I'm innocent,' I muttered, crawling on all fours round my
prison, regardless of the filth my hands and knees encountered.
'I'm innocent, it's quite easy.'

But suddenly I stopped short and stayed motionless, thinking.
It was easy; therefore no triumph, but a defeat. And was I truly
innocent? I had caused suffering. In my best moments I had
remained indifferent to suffering, I had ignored it. Sin had been
indissolubly wedded to my life, and not to mine alone: my fellows
had caused me to suffer and were causing others to suffer: my
fellows ignored my suffering and even approved of it.

The world which I had condemned did no more than remind me
of its existence by causing me to suffer. And what was this world—
a multitude in chaos, an ordered multitude, a single being, a
whole? What were the feathers on the arrow, heron or jay? What
was the poison on its tip, snake-venom or plant? Knowledge alone
could not create an acceptable bond between me and the world:
it could only show the world to be alien and indifferent, the
source of pain. I could hate it easily enough, but I had never tried
to love it. That was less easy. Did not everything that had hap-

pened to me and everything I had done go to prove that knowledge
and experience could bring me only hatred and fear of the world,
and that I must try something else? Did they not show that the
world itself was impelling me through suffering towards a course
that I should not otherwise have contemplated—the effort to love
and forgive it? But since I was a part of the world, with everything
that I was and did, then my love and forgiveness were the world's
own love and forgiveness, which it was teaching me in this harsh
fashion, the only one I was capable of understanding. And if to
love and forgive the world could bring me comfort and joy, was
not this the proof of its own love and forgiveness? Whence did I ac-
quire the power to love and forgive except from the world, from
life itself, which had bestowed it on me, ready for my use when I
was ready to use it? . . . And this was it, the sense and meaning of
the universe: it was love. This was where all the turns of my life
had been leading me. And now everything was truly simple, revealed with a limped clarity to my eyes as though in a flash of light
illuminating the world from end to end, but after which the darkness could never return. Why had I needed to search so long?
Why had I expected a teaching that would come from outside
myself. Why had I expected the world to justify itself to me, and
prove its meaning and purity? It was for me to justify the world
by loving and forgiving it, to discover its meaning through love,
to purify it through forgiveness. . . . I was on my knees and tears
were running down my cheeks. How was I to give thanks, and
what name was I to use? 'God,' I murmured, 'God.' How else
should I address Him? O Universe? O Heap? O Whole? As
'Father' or 'Mother'? I might as well call him 'Uncle'. As 'Lord'?
I might as well say, 'Dear Sir,' or 'Dear Comrade'. How could I say
'Lord' to the air I breathed and my own lungs which breathed the
air? 'My child?' But He contained me, preceded me, created me.
'Thou' is his name, to which 'God' may be added. For 'I' and 'me'
are no more than a pause between the immensity of the universe
which is *Him* and the very depth of our self, which is also *Him*.
Adoration burns away all contradictions, and paradox is its support. The horror of evil impels us to adoration, for God is fearful and horrible and terrifying. Tenderness impels us to adoration
because God is tenderness; and pity no less, because God suffers.
And love is the act of worship. I was crushed with fear, shattered
with pity, rent with the grace and innocence of this universe in
which I was plunged, of which I was made, and which had grown

its flower in my heart, in that quivering, immobile flame, inexhaustible and always spreading. God had been before my eyes from the beginning, I had needed only to speak His name: before me, around me and within me: I had needed only to speak *His* name, which meant to fear and love him, to worship him in love and holy fear.

I was now serene of spirit, and I could have said nothing of what I knew or felt or did except the word *yes*.

POINTS FOR DISCUSSION

1. Read the quotation from Paul Tillich on page 114. What similarities do you notice between the idea of Tillich and the experience of Sebastian?

2. Compare the experience of Sebastian with the experience of Grandier in the extract from John Whiting's play *The Devils* on page 115.

(b) *Part of a conversation between Sebastian, after his release from prison, and his brother Erasmus, who is still a Party member*

'You've been through so much,' he said. 'Torture, starvation, terror and darkness—they've made you mentally ill. Cellini in his Autobiography describes the visions he began to see in prison, for similar reasons. It's a psycho-physiological reaction which now you're making too much of.'

I pointed out that I was now free and normally fed, but that my whole life was still conditioned by those experiences. In any case I had seen no visions. He leaned forward and said with malice:

'Perhaps you're still mad!'

I said that I had had time enough in prison to examine every possibility of doubt. Did he think I was lacking in a sense of reality? I cherished no illusions; I believed in no myth.

'You should visit a psychiatrist,' he said. 'He'll tell you that these fantasies of yours are simply the desire to return to the womb, to be reconciled to the mother—and don't forget what our mother has meant to you! Religious concepts are nothing but a form of obsessional neurosis, wishful thinking—infantilism transferred from a child-parent relationship to an adult-world relationship. You're defending yourself against the cruelty and outrageousness of the world by taking refuge in an *amentia*, or as the English say, a fool's paradise.'

I reminded him that I had said nothing about a Divine Being, or an all-good Deity, or any other, better form of life. I had said nothing about the world that he did not already know. It was a matter of our personal attitude, but less an intellectual position than a plan of action. In any case, was the value of any mental or practical activity diminished by the fact that its origin, or nature, was psycho-sexual? If sacred love was sexual in origin, did this diminish it? Moreover the sense of human solidarity, of being part of a group, was not at all sexual in origin. I had felt this during the war, and on the day when we prisoners had been driven out naked into the bitter wind. It was this sense of solidarity which had to be disseminated throughout the world.

'But you're giving the world the name of God, which is monstrous!' cried Erasmus.

I asked him if it was monstrous of me to call him Erasmus. I used the name of God because it was a way of directing towards the world all the worship, veneration and prayer which our forebears had devoted to gods growing increasingly less circumscribed; until they became the God of the monotheistic religions, defined by the universe, or by evil, or by his own goodness and perfection or by reason. Erasmus burst out:

'You must be mad! Do you mean that this God of yours is not perfect?'

'Yes, He is perfect, but He is also terrible and evil. He is both perfect and imperfect. He is all things, and He confines himself to none.'

'So that I am entitled to hate and despise Him!'

'If you choose. You may worship Him, or hate Him, or ignore Him. . . . Are you really looking for an answer, or don't you care? Are we just chatting to pass the time and prove how intellectual we are? When you can't stand it any longer you'll find the key in yourself, and the strength as well. Are you simply a piddling intellectual who sits drinking coffee and saying, "What's to become of

us, there are no values, where are we going?" and then goes off to
the office or home to the family—or are you a man? Crises are
meant to be mastered. Values have to be broken down until we
come to the solid rock that underlies them, the point of Archi-
medes, the thing in all our hearts which is God and love. It has
to be shouted aloud, for there are no *values*, there is only *one
value* from which all others spring, and it is in ourselves, the living,
active human heart, striving and offering itself. So long as that
is so we may call the universe by the name of God. So long as it is
so, we shall know that God exists; for He is the love in our hearts,
He is we who love and He is the world that we love.'

Erasmus smiled slowly.

'Well! So my brother's a prophet!' He said it ironically, yet
with a kind of tenderness.

'Never mind about me. Think of what I've been saying. It
wasn't me speaking—for a moment I was nothing but the uvula in
the throat of God,' I said, still rather angrily. Erasmus sat down
again and burst out laughing.

'And so the truth has been revealed to us, the inhabitants of
this tiny, cooling satellite of a tenth-rate star in the stews of one of
the lesser galaxies! But that is what is called geocentrism or an-
thropocentrism. It's rather out-of-date!'

I said that he seemed to be mistaking it for a problem of topo-
graphy, when in fact there was no kind of centre that made sense,
whether it was Moscow or Paris, or our galaxy or any other. All
that was beside the point. The centre was everywhere, in my
heart and in his, and in the heart of every other mother's son.

'And God is a demented monster?' said Erasmus, speaking for
the first time with a kind of satisfied serenity.

'God is everything. He is also composed of volcanoes, cancerous
growths and tapeworms. But if you think that justifies you in
jumping into the crater of an active volcano, or wallowing in despair and crime and death, or inoculating yourself with a virus—
well, go ahead. You're like a fish that asks, "Do you mean to say
God isn't only water. He's dry land as well?" To which the answer
is, "Yes, my dear fish. He's dry land as well, but if you go climbing
on to dry land you'll be sorry." '

POINTS FOR DISCUSSION

1. What do you think of Erasmus's comments that Sebastian's experience is due to exhaustion and to mental illness? It it something to be cured by a psychiatrist as he suggests?

2. 'Religious concepts are nothing but a form of ... infantilism transferred from a child-parent relationship to an adult-world relationship.' Discuss what Erasmus means by this comment. Summarize Sebastian's reply to this particular criticism.

3. Erasmus expresses the natural protest of the orthodox when he says, 'But you're giving the world the name of God, which is monstrous!' Do you agree with Erasmus? Is there anything in (*a*) the New Testament or (*b*) the Old Testament which seems to support Sebastian's conception of God?

4. Later on in the book Sebastian is accused of being a 'pantheist'. Discuss the meaning of the word 'pantheist' and decide whether you agree with this critic or not.

5. What do you think of Sebastian's assertion that 'God is in everything. He is also composed of volcanoes, cancerous growths, and tapeworms? (It might be interesting here to look at the Savage's remarks at the end of the passage from *Brave New World* on page 19).

15. CHARLES WILLIAMS

DESCENT INTO HELL

CHARLES WILLIAMS (1886-1945) worked for the Oxford University Press in London and, during the war, in Oxford. For many years he gave evening lectures on literature for the London County Council, and while at Oxford he gave tutorials and lectures to undergraduates. He wrote a great deal in a very wide variety of fields, which include poetry, drama, the novel, literary criticism, and theology.

Williams is one of those writers who attract a small number of enthusiastic devotees rather than a wide public. His novels, although fascinating to many people (*Many Dimensions* is perhaps his best known), are complex both in thought and expression, and his poetry is extremely obscure; he never succeeded in finding a style which exactly suited his purposes. But the impact of his personality as a teacher and as a friend was immense, and while at Oxford he became the central figure of a literary circle which included such people as C. S. Lewis. Nevill Coghill, and J. R. R. Tolkien, and his influence was also strongly felt by the younger generation of the time, as John Wain describes in his autobiography *Sprightly Running*.

Perhaps this suggests that he was merely a 'writer's writer'—and this may indeed be the case. But he undoubtedly had an extraordinary spiritual insight and sensitivity. T. S. Eliot wrote of him after his death: 'There are many good Christians today who believe in spiritual reality but have no experience of it; their Christianity is rather an aspiration than an awareness. To be brought face to face with what Williams *saw* is a need for those who call themselves Christians as it is for everyone else.'

This extract comes from his novel *Descent into Hell*, and illustrates how Williams interprets Christ's command that we should 'bear one another's burdens'. Such acts of 'substitution' or 'exchange', as he calls them, are symptoms of a profound truth about human life and ideally involve much more than isolated acts of kindness or sympathy. In his view, Christianity does not so much tell us how to behave as tell us *how things are*; it does not so much tell us that we should live *for* others as that we do in fact live *from* others, i.e. that our lives at all levels are inextricably bound together in interdependence. So 'bearing one another's burdens' is not simply a series of good deeds, but an acceptance of a truth which he saw as a pattern running throughout human life, in human relationships and even in the structure of society

itself. He did not in fact need to bring in Christianity to support his
belief that we are 'members one of another'.

In the extract, Peter Stanhope is a well-known poet attending a
rehearsal of an amateur production of one of his plays, in which Adela
has an important part; Mrs. Parry is the producer.

Substitution and exchange

Someone sat down in the next chair. She looked; it was Stanhope. Mrs. Parry and Adela concluded their discussion. The
rehearsal began again. Stanhope said: 'You were, of course,
quite right.'

She turned her head towards him, gravely. 'You meant it like
that then?' she asked.

'Certainly I meant it like that,' he said, 'more like that anyhow. Do you suppose I want each line I made to march so many
paces to the right, with a meditation between each? But even if
I could interfere, it'd only get more mixed then ever. Better keep
it all of a piece.'

She said suddenly, 'Would you read it to me again one day? Is
it too absurd to ask you?'

'Of course I'll read it,' he said. 'Why not? If you'd like it. And
now in exchange tell me what's bothering you.'

Taken aback, she stared at him, and stammered on her answer.
'But—but——' she began.

He looked at the performers. 'Miss Hunt is determined to turn
me into the solid geometry of the emotions,' he said. 'But—but—
tell me why you always look so about you and what you are looking for.'

'Do I?' she asked hesitatingly. He turned a serious gaze on her
and her own eyes turned away before it. He said, 'There's nothing
worth quite so much vigilance or anxiety. Watchfulness, but not
anxiety, not fear. You let it into yourself when you fear so; and
whatever it is, it's less than your life.'

'You talk as if life were good,' she said.

'It's either good or evil,' he answered, 'and you can't decide that
by counting incidents on your fingers. The decision is of another
kind. But don't let's be abstract. Will you tell me what it is
bothers you?'

She said, 'It sounds too silly.'

Stanhope paused, and in the silence there came to them Mrs. Parry's voice carefully enunciating a grand ducal speech to Hugh Prescott. The measured syllables fell in globed detachment at their feet, and Stanhope waved a hand outwards.

'Well,' he said, 'if you think it sounds sillier than that. God is good; if I hadn't been here they might have done the Tempest. Consider—"Yea—all which—it inher–it—shall dissolve. And—like this—insub–stantial pag–eant fa–ded." O certainly God is good. So what about telling me?'

'I have a trick,' she said steadily. 'of meeting an exact likeness of myself in the street.' And as if she hated herself for saying it, she turned sharply on him. 'There!' she exclaimed. 'Now you know. You know exactly. And what will you say?'

Her eyes burned at him; he received their fury undisturbed, saying, 'You mean exactly that?' and she nodded. 'Well,' he went on mildly, 'it's not unknown. Goethe met himself once—upon the road to Weimar, I think. But he didn't make it a habit. How long has this been happening?'

'All my life,' she answered. 'At intervals—long intervals, I know. Months and years sometimes, only it's quicker now. O, it's insane—no one could believe it, and yet it's there.'

'It's your absolute likeness?' he asked.

'It's me,' she repeated. 'It comes from a long way off, and it comes up towards me, and I'm terrified—terrified—one day it'll come on and meet me. It hasn't so far; it's turned away or disappeared. But it won't always; it'll come right up to me—and then I shall go mad or die.'

'Why?' he asked quickly, and she answered at once, 'Because I'm afraid. Dreadfully afraid.'

'But that,' he said, 'I don't quite understand. You have friends; haven't you asked one of them to carry your fear?'

'Carry my fear!' she said, sitting rigid in her chair, so that her arms, which had lain so lightly, pressed now into the basket-work and her long firm hands gripped it as if they strangled her own heart. 'How can anyone else carry my fear? Can anyone else see it and have to meet it?'

Still, in that public place, leaning back easily as if they talked of casual things, he said. 'You're mixing up two things. Think a moment, and you'll see. The meeting it—that's one thing, and we can leave it till you're rid of the other. It's the fear we're talking about. Has no one ever relieved you of that? Haven't you ever asked them to?'

She said: 'You haven't understood, of course.... I was a fool.... Let's forget it. Isn't Mrs. Parry efficient?'

'Extremely,' he answered. 'And God redeem her. But nicely. Will you tell me whether you've any notion of what I'm talking about? And if not, will you let me do it for you?'

She attended reluctantly, as if to attend were an unhappy duty she owed him, as she had owed others to others and tried to fulfil them. She said politely, 'Do it for me?'

'It can be done, you know,' he went on. 'It's surprisingly simple. And if there's no one else you care to ask, why not use me? I'm here at your disposal, and we could so easily settle it that way. Then you needn't fear it, at least, and then again for the meeting—that might be a very different business if you weren't distressed.'

'But how can I not be afraid?' she asked. 'It's hellish nonsense to talk like that. I suppose that's rude, but——'

'It's no more nonsense than your own story,' he said. 'That isn't; very well, this isn't. We all know what fear and trouble are. Very well—when you leave here you'll think of yourself that I've taken this particular trouble over instead of you. You'd do as much for me if I needed it, or for any one. And I will give myself to it. I'll think of what comes to you, and imagine it, and know it, and be afraid of it. And then, you see, you won't.'

She looked at him as if she were beginning to understand that at any rate he thought he was talking about a reality, and as she did so something of her feeling for him returned. It was, after all, Peter Stanhope who was talking to her like this. Peter Stanhope was a great poet. Were great poets liars? No. But they might be mistaken. Yes; so might she. She said, very doubtfully: 'But I don't understand. It isn't *your*—you haven't seen it. How can you——'

He indicated the rehearsal before them. 'Come,' he said, 'if you like *that*, will you tell me that I must see in order to know? That's not pride, and if it were it wouldn't matter. Listen—when you go from here, when you're alone, when you think you'll be afraid, let me put myself in your place, and be afraid instead of you.' He sat up and leaned towards her. 'It's so easy,' he went on, 'easy for both of us. It needs only the act. For what can be simpler than for you to think to yourself that since I am here to be troubled instead of you, therefore you needn't be troubled? And what can be easier than for me to carry a little while a burden that isn't mine?'

She said, still perplexed at a strange language: 'But how can I cease to be troubled? Will it leave off coming because I pretend it wants you? Is it your resemblance that hurries up the street?'

'It is not,' he said, 'and you shall not pretend at all. The thing itself you may one day meet—never mind that now, but you'll be free from all distress because that you can pass on to me. Haven't you heard it said that we ought to bear one another's burdens?'

'But that means——' she began, and stopped.

'I know,' Stanhope said. 'It means listening sympathetically, and thinking unselfishly, and being anxious about, and so on. Well, I don't say a word against all that; no doubt it helps. But I think when Christ or St. Paul, or whoever said *bear*, or whatever he Aramaically said instead of *bear*, he meant something much more like carrying a parcel instead of someone else. To bear a burden is precisely to carry it instead of. If you're still carrying yours, I'm not carrying it for you—however sympathetic I may be. And anyhow there's no need to introduce Christ, unless you wish. It's a fact of experience. If you give a weight to me, you can't be carrying it yourself; all I'm asking you to do is to notice that blazing truth. It doesn't sound very difficult.'

'And if I could,' she said. 'If I could do—whatever it is you mean, would I? Would I push my burden on to anybody else?'

'Not, if you insist on making a universe for yourself,' he answered. 'If you want to disobey and refuse the laws that are common to us all, if you want to live in pride and division and anger, you can. But if you will be a part of the best of us, and live and laugh and be ashamed with us, then you must be content to be helped. You must give up your burden to someone else and you must carry someone else's burden. I haven't made the universe and it isn't my fault. But I'm sure that this is a law of the universe, and not to give up your parcel is as much to rebel as not to carry another's. You'll find it quite easy if you let yourself do it.'

'And what of my self-respect?' she said.

He laughed at her with tender mockery. 'O, if we are of that kind!' he exclaimed. 'If you want to respect yourself, if to respect yourself you must go clean against the nature of things, if you must refuse the Omnipotence in order to respect yourself, though why you should want so extremely to respect yourself is more than

I can guess, why, go on and respect. Must I apologise for suggesting anything else?'

He mocked her and was silent; for a long while she stared back, still irresolute. He held her; presently he held her at command. A long silence had gone by before he spoke again.

'When you are alone,' he said, 'remember that I am afraid instead of you, and that I have taken over every kind of worry. Think merely that; say to yourself—"he is being worried," and go on. Remember it is mine. If you do not see it, well; if you do, you will not be afraid. And since you are not afraid. . . .'

She stood up. 'I can't imagine not being afraid,' she said.

'But you will not be,' he answered, also rising, certainty in his voice, 'because you will leave all that to me. Will you please me by remembering that absolutely?'

'I am to remember,' she said, and almost broke into a little trembling laugh, 'that you are being worried and terrified instead of me?'

'That I have taken it all over,' he said, 'so there is nothing left for you.'

'And if I see it after all?' she asked.

'But not "after all",' he said. 'The fact remains—but see how different a fact, if it can't be dreaded! As of course it can't—by you. Go now, if you choose, and keep it in your mind till—shall I see you tomorrow? Or ring me up tonight, say about nine, and tell me you are being obedient to the whole fixed nature of things.'

POINTS FOR DISCUSSION

1. We all know the platitude 'A trouble shared is a trouble halved.' To what extent does Stanhope's idea go beyond this?

2. We are told that Christians should be 'members one of another'. Does this mean more than being members of the same group or society? What other examples of this idea can you remember from the New Testament, both with regard to the relationship between human beings, and the relationship between God and Christ?

3. Would you agree with Adela that giving up one's burden is damaging to one's self-respect? What lies behind Stanhope's 'tender mockery' at this point?

4. Is Stanhope's idea a practical proposition and relevant to everyday life, or is it just an idealistic exaggeration of what Christ meant?

5. Williams said that our greatest temptation was to limit the operation of 'bearing one another's burdens' to situations where our emotions were sympathetically involved. Do you agree with him? Consider the following 'unemotional' definition of Christian love: 'Love is the accurate estimate and supply of the needs of others.'

16. EVELYN WAUGH

THE LOVED ONE

EVELYN WAUGH (1903–1966) was educated at Lancing College and at
Hertford College, Oxford. His career as a novelist began in 1928 with
the publication of *Decline and Fall*, a comic and mildly satirical account
of the adventures of a young man unjustly sent down from Oxford.
There followed over the next few years *Vile Bodies* (1930), *Black Mis-
chief* (1932), *A Handful of Dust* (1934) and *Scoop* (1938), all of which
satirized various aspects of life, both at home and abroad, between the
wars, but in particular the manners and values of the English upper-
middle classes in the late twenties and early thirties.

There is however far more to Waugh than the brilliance of his humour
and the elegance of his style. He became a Roman Catholic in 1930 and
his faith undoubtedly became the mainspring of his creativity, as can
be seen in particular in his later novels such as *Brideshead Revisited*
(1945) and the trilogy *Sword of Honour*, which was published in its three
separate parts between 1952 and 1961.

The Loved One (1948) is a satire, both gruesome and amusing, on
the American funeral industry. It grew out of observations made by
Waugh while visiting Forest Lawn Memorial Park in Los Angeles,
which appears as Whispering Glades in the novel. Describing his visit in
an article in *Life* magazine in 1947 he wrote:

> Forest Lawn has consciously turned its back on the 'old customs of
> Death', the grim traditional alternatives of Heaven and Hell, and
> promises immediate eternal happiness for all its inmates.... The
> body does not decay; it lives on, more chic in death than ever
> before ... the soul goes straight from the Slumber Room to
> Paradise, where it enjoys an endless infancy.

The story concerns Dennis Barlow, a young English poet, who has
come to Hollywood intending to work in films, but who has taken a
job in The Happy Hunting Ground, a pets' cemetery. He is staying
at the home of another Englishman, Sir Francis Hinsley, formerly a
distinguished script-writer, whose reputation has decreased as his age
increases and his powers decline. Sir Francis commits suicide by hanging
himself and Dennis visits Whispering Glades to make arrangements for
the funeral.

Whispering Glades

Dennis passed through and opening the door marked
'Inquiries' found himself in a raftered banqueting-hall. 'The
Hindu Love-song' was here also, gently discoursed from the dark-
oak panelling. A young lady rose from a group of her fellows to
welcome him, one of that new race of exquisite, amiable, efficient
young ladies whom he had met everywhere in the United States.
She wore a white smock and over her sharply supported left breast
was embroidered the words, *Mortuary Hostess*.

'Can I help you in any way?'

'I came to arrange about a funeral.'

'Is it for yourself?'

'Certainly not. Do I look so moribund?'

'Pardon me?'

'Do I look as if I were about to die?'

'Why, no. Only many of our friends like to make Before Need
Arrangements. Will you come this way?'

She led him from the hall into a soft passage. The *décor* here
was Georgian. The 'Hindu Love-song' came to its end and was
succeeded by the voice of a nightingale. In a little chintzy parlour
he and his hostess sat down to make their arrangements.

'I must first record the Essential Data.'

He told her his name and Sir Francis's.

'Now, Mr. Barlow, what had you in mind? Embalmment of
course, and after that incineration or not, according to taste. Our
crematory is on scientific principles, the heat is so intense that all
inessentials are volatilized. Some people did not like the thought
that ashes of the casket and clothing were mixed with the Loved
One's. Normal disposal is by inhumement, entombment, inurn-
ment or immurement, but many people just lately prefer insarco-
phagusment. That is *very* individual. The casket is placed inside
a sealed sarcophagus, marble or bronze, and rests permanently
above ground in a niche in the mausoleum, with or without a
personal stained-glass window above. That, of course, is for those
with whom price it not a primary consideration.'

'We want my friend buried.'

'This is not your first visit to Whispering Glades?'

'Yes.'

'Then let me explain the Dream. The Park is zoned. Each zone has its own name and appropriate Work of Art. Zones of course vary in price and within the zones the prices vary according to their proximity to the Work of Art. We have single sites as low as fifty dollars. That is in Pilgrim's Rest, a zone we are just developing behind the Crematory fuel dump. The most costly are those on Lake Isle. They range about 1,000 dollars. Then there is Lovers' Nest, zoned about a very, very beautiful marble replica of Rodin's famous statue, the Kiss. We have double plots there at 750 dollars the pair. Was your Loved One married?'

'No.'

'What was his business?'

'He was a writer.'

'Ah, then Poets' Corner would be the place for him. We have many of our foremost literary names there, either in person or as Before Need Reservations. You are no doubt acquainted with the works of Amelia Bergson?'

'I know of them.'

'We sold Miss Bergson a Before Need Reservation only yesterday, under the statue of the prominent Greek poet Homer. I could put your friend right next to her. But perhaps you would like to see the zone before deciding.'

'I want to see everything.'

'There certainly is plenty to see. I'll have one of our guides take you round just as soon as we have all the Essential Data, Mr. Barlow. Was your Loved One of any special religion?'

'An agnostic.'

'We have two non-sectarian churches in the Park and a number of non-sectarian pastors. Jews and Catholics seem to prefer to make their own arrangements.'

'I believe Sir Ambrose Abercrombie is planning a special service.'

'Oh, was your Loved One in films, Mr. Barlow? In that case he ought to be in Shadowland.'

'I think he would prefer to be with Homer and Miss Bergson.'

'Then the University Church would be most convenient. We like to save the Waiting Ones a long procession. I presume the Loved One was Caucasian?'

'No, why did you think that? He was purely English.'

'English are purely Caucasian, Mr. Barlow. This is a restricted park. The Dreamer has made that rule for the sake of the Waiting

Ones. In their time of trial they prefer to be with their own people.'

'I think I understand. Well, let me assure you Sir Francis was quite white.'

As he said this there came vividly into Dennis's mind that image which lurked there, seldom out of sight for long; the sack of body suspended and the face above it with eyes red and horribly starting from their sockets, the cheeks mottled in indigo like the marbled end-papers of a ledger and the tongue swollen and protruding like an end of black sausage.

'Let us now decide on the casket.'

They went to the show-rooms where stood coffins of every shape and material; the nightingale still sang in the cornice.

'The two-piece lid is most popular for gentlemen Loved Ones. Only the upper part is then exposed to view.'

'Exposed to view?'

'Yes, when the Waiting Ones come to take leave.'

'But, I say, I don't think that will quite do. I've seen him. He's terribly disfigured, you know.'

'If there are any special little difficulties in the case you must mention them to our cosmeticians. You will be seeing one of them before you leave. They have never failed yet.'

Dennis made no hasty choice. He studied all that was for sale; even the simplest of these coffins, he humbly recognized, outshone the most gorgeous product of the Happier Hunting Ground and when he approached the 2,000-dollar level—and these were not the costliest—he felt himself in the Egypt of the Pharaohs. At length he decided on a massive chest of walnut with bronze enrichments and an interior of quilted satin. Its lid, as recommended, was in two parts.

'You are sure that they will be able to make him presentable?'

'We had a Loved One last month who was found drowned. He had been in the ocean a month and they only identified him by his wrist-watch. They fixed that stiff,' said the hostess disconcertingly lapsing from the high diction she had hitherto employed, 'so he looked like it was his wedding day. The boys up there surely know their job. Why, if he'd sat on an atom bomb, they'd make him presentable.'

'That's very comforting.'

'I'll say it is.' And then slipping on her professional manner again as though it were a pair of glasses, she resumed. 'How will the Loved One be attired? We have our own tailoring section. Sometimes after a very long illness there are not suitable clothes available and sometimes the Waiting Ones think it a waste of a good suit. You see, we can fit a Loved One out very reasonably as a casket-suit does not have to be designed for hard wear and in cases where only the upper part is exposed for leave-taking there is no need for more than jacket and vest. Something dark is best to set off the flowers.'

Dennis was entirely fascinated. At length he said: 'Sir Francis was not much of a dandy. I doubt of his having anything quite suitable for casket wear. But in Europe, I think, we usually employ a shroud.'

'Oh, we have shrouds too. I'll show you some.'

The hostess led him to a set of sliding shelves like a sacristy chest where vestments are stored, and drawing one out revealed a garment such as Dennis had never seen before. Observing his interest she held it up for his closer inspection. It was in appearance like a suit of clothes, buttoned in front but open down the back; the sleeves hung loose, open at the seam; half an inch of linen appeared at the cuff and the V of the waistcoat was similarly filled; a knotted bow-tie emerged from the opening of a collar which also lay as though slit from behind. It was the apotheosis of the 'dickey.'

'A speciality of our own,' she said, 'though it is now widely imitated. The idea came from the quick-change artists of vaudeville. It enables one to dress the Loved Ones without disturbing the pose.'

'Most remarkable. I believe that is just the article we require.'

'With or without trousers?'

'What precisely is the advantage of trousers?'

'For the Slumber-Room wear. It depends whether you wish the leave-taking to be on the chaise-longue or in the casket.'

'Perhaps I had better see the Slumber Room before deciding.'

'You're welcome.'

She led him out to the hall and up a staircase. The nightingale had now given place to the organ and strains of Handel followed them to the Slumber Floor. Here she asked a colleague, 'Which room have we free?'

'Only Daffodil.'

'This way, Mr. Barlow.'

They passed many closed doors of pickled oak until at length she opened one and stood aside for him to enter. He found a little room, brightly furnished and papered. It might have been part of a luxurious modern country club in all its features save one. Bowls of flowers stood disposed about a chintz sofa and on the sofa lay what seemed to be the wax effigy of an elderly woman dressed as though for an evening party. Her white gloved hands held a bouquet and on her nose glittered a pair of rimless pince-nez.

'Oh,' said his guide, 'how foolish of me. We've come into Primrose by mistake. This,' she added superfluously, 'is occupied.'

'Yes.'

'The leave-taking is not till the afternoon but we had better go before one of the cosmeticians finds us. They like to make a few final adjustments before Waiting Ones are admitted. Still, it gives you an idea of the chaise-longue arrangement. We usually recommend the casket half-exposure for gentlemen because the legs never look so well.'

She led him out.

'Will there be many for the leave-taking?'

'Yes, I rather think so, a great many.'

'Then you had better have a suite with an ante-room. The Orchid Room is the best. Shall I make a reservation for that?'

'Yes, do.'

'And the half-exposure in the casket, not the chaise-longue?'

'Not the chaise-longue.'

She led him back towards the reception room.

'It may seem a little strange to you, Mr. Barlow, coming on a Loved One unexpectedly in that way.'

'I confess it did a little.'

'You will find it quite different on the day. The leave-taking is a very, very great source of consolation. Often the Waiting Ones last saw their Loved One on a bed of pain surrounded by all the gruesome concomitants of the sick room or the hospital. Here they see them as they knew them in bouyant life, transfigured with peace and happiness. At the funeral they have time only for a last look as they file past. Here in the Slumber Room they can stand as long as they like photographing a last beautiful memory on the mind.'

She spoke, he observed, partly by the book, in the words of the Dreamer, partly in her own brisk language. They were back in the reception room now and she spoke briskly. 'Well, I guess I've

got all I want out of you, Mr. Barlow, except your signature to
the order and a deposit.'

Dennis had come prepared for this. It was part of the Happier
Hunting Ground procedure. He paid her 500 dollars and took
her receipt.

'Now one of our cosmeticians is waiting to see you and get *her*
Essential Data, but before we part may I interest you in our
Before Need Provision Arrangements?'

'Everything about Whispering Glades interests me profoundly,
but that aspect, perhaps, less than others.'

'The benefits of the plan are twofold'—she was speaking by
the book now with a vengeance—'financial and psychological.
You, Mr. Barlow, are now approaching your optimum earning
phase. You are no doubt making provision of many kinds for your
future—investments, insurance policies and so forth. You plan
to spend your declining days in security but have you considered
what burdens you may not be piling up for those you leave behind? Last month, Mr. Barlow, a husband and wife were here con-
sulting us about Before Need Provision. They were prominent
citizens in the prime of life with two daughters just budding into
womanhood. They heard all particulars, they were impressed and
said they would return in a few days time to complete arrangements. Only next day those two passed on, Mr. Barlow, in an
automobile accident, and instead of them there came two dis-
traught orphans to ask what arrangements their parents had
made. We were obliged to inform them that *no* arrangements had
been made. In the hour of their greatest need those children were
left comfortless. How different it would have been had we been
able to say to them: "Welcome to all the Happiness of Whispering Glades." '

'Yes, but you know I haven't any children. Besides I am a
foreigner. I have no intention of dying here.'

'Mr. Barlow, you are afraid of death.'

'No, I assure you.'

'It is a natural instinct, Mr. Barlow, to shrink from the unknown.
But if you discuss it openly and frankly you remove morbid reflections. That is one of the things the psycho-analysts have taught
us. Bring your dark fears into the light of the common day of the
common man, Mr. Barlow. Realize that death is not a private
tragedy of your own but the general lot of man. As Hamlet so
beautifully writes: "Know that death is common; all that live

must die." Perhaps you think it morbid and even dangerous to give thought to this subject, Mr. Barlow; the contrary has been proved by scientific investigation. Many people let their vital energy lag prematurely and their earning capacity diminish simply through fear of death. By removing that fear they actually increase their expectation of life. Choose now, at leisure and in health, the form of final preparation you require, pay for it while you are best able to do so, shed all anxiety. Pass the buck, Mr. Barlow; Whispering Glades can take it.'

POINTS FOR DISCUSSION

1. Waugh lamented that Forest Lawn deprived death of its dignity. Judging from his description of Whispering Glades, would you agree with him?

2. What particular attitudes to death are implied by the existence of such places as Whispering Glades?

3. It has been said that death is the great taboo subject today, as sex once was. Do you agree? What euphemisms for death are used in this extract? What euphemisms do we use for death? What do these imply?

4. What kinds of civilizations will tend to cover up what Waugh once called 'the mystery and enormity of death'?

5. Whispering Glades seems to be directed towards taking the grief out of death. Do you think this is a good aim?

6. 'To a non-religious reader, however, the patrons and proprietors of Whispering Glades seem more sensible than the priest-guided Evelyn Waugh. What the former are trying to do is, after all, to gloss over physical death with smooth lawns and soothing rites; but for the Catholic the fact of death is not to be feared at all....'[1] Do you agree with this comment?

[1] Edmund Wilson, *Classics and Commercials: A Literary Chronicle of the Forties.*

17. FYODOR DOSTOEVSKY

THE BROTHERS KARAMAZOV

DOSTOEVSKY was born in Moscow in 1821. As a young man he embarked upon the army career for which his education at the army engineering school in St. Petersburg had prepared him, but in 1844 he resigned his commission and began work upon his first novel *Poor Folk*, which was a considerable success. At about this time he joined a group of revolutionary socialists and campaigned actively with them for various social reforms, including the abolition of serfdom and freedom from censorship. In 1849 he was arrested and, together with others of his group, was sentenced to death. News of a reprieve arrived with dramatic suddenness while they were being prepared for execution, and the sentence was commuted to one of four years in Siberia followed by service in the army in the ranks. Dostoevsky left the army on health grounds (he suffered from epilepsy) in 1858 and returned to St. Petersburg and devoted himself to his writing. In this period he wrote six long novels, including *Crime and Punishment*, *The Idiot*, and *The Devils*. *The Brothers Karamazov*, from which these extracts are taken, was his last novel and was published a year before his death in 1881.

Dostoevsky was one of the greatest creative artists of the nineteenth century. He thought deeply on the social, political, and religious problems affecting his times, and in his novels he deals profoundly and fearlessly with these themes. Of his preliminary ideas for *The Brothers Karamazov* he said, 'The main question that will be discussed ... is one that has worried me, consciously or unconsciously, all my life—the existence of God.' He calls the legend of the Grand Inquisitor (recounted in these extracts) 'the culminating point of my literary activity'. This famous story has a powerful and mysterious appeal; what Dostoevsky meant by it has been variously interpreted; he is not an easy writer to understand, and often perversely, or at any rate paradoxically, puts the case of the other side more strongly than his own. In this story he was clearly attacking the institutions and political movements of his own time, but it has a universal appeal which transcends the problems of nineteenth-century Russia.

Ivan and Alyosha are sons of Fyodor Karamazov, a mean and dissolute Russian landowner. They have not seen each other since childhood until Ivan, a writer with some revolutionary ideas, returns to his home town to help in settling a family dispute. Alyosha is a novice in a monastery. At the time of their conversation, which takes place in the inn where Ivan is staying, both men are in their early twenties.

All these extracts should be read before attempting the points for discussion.

(a) *In the course of their conversation together, Ivan is attempting to explain to his brother the beliefs by which he lives, and he has just delivered an impassioned outburst against the evil and cruelty of the world, which he says he 'cannot accept'. When Alyosha at length reminds Ivan that ultimate harmony, which he so desires, is in fact brought about by the innocent blood of Christ, Ivan replies that he has written a poem called The Grand Inquisitor and he goes on to give an account of it*

'The action of my poem takes place in Spain, in Seville, during the most terrible time of the Inquisition, when fires were lighted every day throughout the land to the glory of God and

> *In the splendid autos-da-fé*
> *Wicked heretics were burnt.*

Oh, of course, this was not the second coming when, as he promised, he would appear at the end of time in all his heavenly glory, and which would be as sudden "as the lightning cometh out of the east, and shineth even unto the west". No, all he wanted was to visit his children only for a moment and just where the stakes of the heretics were crackling in the flames. In his infinite mercy he once more walked among men in the semblance of man as he had walked among men for thirty-three years fifteen centuries ago. He came down into the hot "streets and lanes" of the southern city just at the moment when, a day before, nearly a hundred heretics had been burnt all at once by the cardinal, the Grand Inquisitor, *ad majorem gloriam Dei* in "a magnificent auto da fé", in the presence of the king, the court, the knights, the cardinals, and the fairest ladies of the Court and the whole population of Seville. He appeared quietly, inconspicuously, but everyone—and that is why it is so strange—recognized him. That might have been one of the finest passages in my poem—I mean, why they recognized him. The people are drawn to him by an irresistible force, they surround him, they throng about him, they follow him. He walks among them in silence with a gentle smile of infinite compassion. The sun of love burns in his heart, rays of Light, of Enlightenment, and of Power stream from his eyes and, pouring over the people, stir their hearts with responsive love. He stretches forth his hands to them, blesses them, and a healing virtue comes from contact with him, even with his garments. An old man, blind from childhood, cries out to him from the midst of the crowd, "O Lord, heal me so that I may see thee," and it is as though scales fell from his eyes, and the blind man sees him. The people weep and kiss the ground upon which he walks. Children scatter flowers before him, sing and cry out to him: "Hosannah!" "It is he, it is he himself," they all repeat. "It must be he, it can be no one but he." He stops on the steps of the Cathedral of Seville at the moment when a child's little, open white coffin is brought in with weeping into the church: in it lies a girl of seven, the only daughter of a prominent citizen. The dead child is covered with flowers. "He will raise up your child," people shout from the crowd to the weeping mother. The canon, who has come out to meet the coffin, looks on perplexed and knits his brows. But presently a cry of the dead child's mother is heard. She throws herself at his feet. "If it is thou," she cries, holding out her hands to him, "then raise my child from the dead!" The funeral cortège halts. The coffin is lowered on to the steps at his feet. He gazes with compassion and his lips once again utter softly the words, "Talitha cumi"—"and the damsel arose". The little girl rises in the coffin, sits up, and looks around her with surprise in her smiling, wide-open eyes. In her hands she holds the nosegay of white roses with which she lay in her coffin. There are cries, sobs, and confusion among the people, and it is at that very moment that the Cardinal himself, the Grand Inquisitor, passes by the cathedral in the square. He is an old man of nearly ninety, tall and erect, with a shrivelled face and sunken eyes, from which, though, a light like a fiery spark still gleams. Oh, he is not wearing his splended cardinal robes in which he appeared before the people the day before, when the enemies of the Roman faith were being burnt—no, at that moment he is wearing only his old, coarse, monk's cassock. He is followed at a distance by his sombre assistants and his slaves and his "sacred" guard. He stops in front of the crowd and watches from a distance. He sees everything. He sees the coffin set down at *his* feet, he sees the young girl raised from the dead, and his face darkens. He knits his grey, beetling brows and his eyes flash with an ominous fire. He stretches forth his finger and commands the guards to seize *him*. And so great is his power and so accustomed are the people to obey him, so humble and submissive are they to his will, that the crowd immediately makes way for the guards and, amid the death-like hush that descends upon the square, they lay hands upon *him* and lead him away. The crowd, like one man, at once bows down to the ground before the old Inquisitor, who blesses them in silence and passes on. The guards take their Prisoner to the dark, narrow, vaulted prison in the old building of the Sacred Court and lock him in there. The day passes and night falls, the dark, hot and "breathless" Seville night. The air is "heavy with the scent of laurel and lemon". Amid the profound darkness, the iron door of the prison is suddenly opened and the old Grand Inquisitor himself slowly enters the prison with a light in his hand. He is alone and the door at once closes behind him. He stops in the doorway and gazes for a long time, for more than a minute, into his face. At last he approaches him slowly, puts the lamp on the table and says to him:

' "Is it you? You?"

'But, receiving no answer, he adds quickly: "Do not answer, be silent. And, indeed, what can you say? I know too well what you would say. Besides, you have no right to add anything to what you have said already in the days of old. Why, then, did you come to meddle with us? For you have come to meddle with us, and you know it. But do you know what is going to happen tomorrow? I know not who you are and I don't want to know: whether it is you or only someone who looks like him, I do not know, but tomorrow I shall condemn you and burn you at the stake as the vilest of heretics, and the same people who today kissed your feet, will at the first sign from me rush to rake up the coals at your stake tomorrow. Do you know that? Yes, perhaps you do know it," he added after a moment of deep reflection without taking his eyes off his prisoner for an instant.'

(b) The Inquisitor reminds Christ of the time when he was tempted by the 'terrible and wise spirit, the spirit of self-destruction and non-existence' in the wilderness

' "Decide yourself who was right—you or he who questioned you then? Call to your mind the first question; its meaning, though not in these words, was this: 'You want to go into the world and you are going empty-handed, with some promise of freedom, which men in their simplicity and their innate lawlessness cannot even comprehend, which they fear and dread—for nothing has ever been more unendurable to man and to human society than freedom! And do you see the stones in this parched and barren desert? Turn them into loaves, and mankind will run after you like a flock of sheep, grateful and obedient, though for ever trembling with fear that you might withdraw your hand and they would no longer have your loaves.' But you did not want to deprive man of freedom and rejected the offer, for, you thought, what sort of freedom is it if obedience is bought with loaves of bread? You replied that man does not live by bread alone, but do you know that for the sake of that earthly bread the spirit of the earth will rise up against you and will join battle with you and conquer you, and all will follow him, crying 'Who is like this beast? He has given us fire from heaven!' Do you know that ages will pass and mankind will proclaim in its wisdom and science that there is no crime and, therefore, no sin, but that there are only hungry people. 'Feed them first and then demand virtue of them!'—that is what they will inscribe on their banner which they will raise against you and which will destroy your temple.

' "And look what you have done further—and all again in the name of freedom! ... Instead of taking possession of men's freedom you multiplied it and burdened the spiritual kingdom of man with its sufferings for ever. You wanted man's free love so that he should follow you freely, fascinated and captivated by you. Instead of the strict ancient law, man had in future to decide for himself with a free heart what is good and what is evil, having only your image before him for guidance. But did it never occur to you that he would at last reject and call in question even your image and your truth, if he were weighed down by so fearful a burden as freedom of choice? They will at last cry aloud that the truth is not in you, for it was impossible to leave them in greater confusion and suffering than you have done by leaving them with so many cares and insoluble problems. It was you yourself, therefore, who laid the foundation for the destruction of your kingdom and you ought not to blame anyone else for it. And yet, is that all that was offered to you? There are three forces, the only three forces that are able to conquer and hold captive for ever the conscience of these weak rebels for their own happiness—these forces are: miracle, mystery, and authority. You rejected all three and yourself set the example for doing so. When the wise and terrible spirit set you on a pinnacle of the temple and said to you: 'If thou be the Son of God, cast thyself down: for it is written, He shall give his angels charge concerning thee: and in their hands they shall bear thee up, lest at any time thou dash thy foot against a stone, and thou shalt prove then how great is thy faith in thy Father.' But, having heard him, you rejected his proposal and did not give way and did not cast yourself down. Oh, of course, you acted proudly and magnificently, like God. But men, the weak, rebellious race of men, are they gods? Oh, you understood perfectly then that in taking one step, in making a move to cast yourself down, you would at once have tempted God and have lost all your faith in him, and you would have been dashed to pieces against the earth which you came to save, and the wise spirit that tempted you would have rejoiced. But, I repeat, are there many like you? And could you really assume for a moment that men, too, could be equal to such a temptation? Is the nature of man such that he can reject a miracle and at the most fearful moments of life, the moments of his most fearful, fundamental and agonizing spiritual problems, stick to the free decision of the heart? Oh, you knew that your great deed would be preserved in books, that it would go down to the end of time and the extreme ends of the earth, and you hoped that, following you, man would remain with God and ask for no miracle. But you did not know that as soon as man rejected miracle he would at once reject God as well, for what man seeks is not so much God as miracles. And since man is unable to carry on without a miracle, he will create new miracles for himself, miracles of his own, and will worship the miracle of the witch-doctor and the sorcery of the wise woman, rebel, heretic and infidel though he is a hundred times over. You did not come down from the cross when they shouted to you, mocking and deriding you: 'If thou be the Son of God, come down from the cross.' You did not come down because, again, you did not want to enslave man by a miracle and because you hungered for a faith based on free will and not on miracles. You hungered for freely given love and not for the servile raptures of the slave before the might that has terrified him once and for all. But here, too, your judgement of men was too high, for they are slaves, though rebels by nature. Look round and judge: fifteen centuries have passed, go and have a look at them: whom have you raised up to yourself? I swear, man has been created a weaker and baser creature than you thought him to be! Can he, can he do what you did? In respecting him so greatly, you acted as though you ceased to feel any compassion for him, for you asked too much of him—you who have loved him more than yourself!" '

(c) *The Inquisitor continues to blame Christ for burdening men with freedom instead of satisfying their basic needs*

' "That was the meaning of the first question in the wilderness, and that was what you rejected in the name of freedom, which you put above everything else. And yet in that question lay hidden the great secret of this world. By accepting 'the loaves', you would have satisfied man's universal and everlasting craving, both as an individual and as mankind as a whole, which can be summed up in the words 'whom shall I worship?' Man, so long as he remains free, has no more constant and agonizing anxiety than to find as quickly as possible someone to worship. But man seeks to worship only what is incontestable, so incontestable, indeed, that all men at once agree to worship it all together. For the chief concern of those miserable creatures is not only to find something that I or someone else can worship, but to find something that all believe in and worship, and the absolutely essential thing is that they should do so *all together*. It is this need for *universal* worship that is the chief torment of every man individually and of mankind as a whole from the beginning of time. For the sake of that universal worship they have put each other to the sword. They have set up gods and called upon each other, 'Give up your gods and come and worship ours, or else death to you and to your gods!' And so it will be to the end of the world, even when the gods have vanished from the earth: they will prostrate themselves before idols just the same. You knew, you couldn't help knowing this fundamental mystery of human nature, but you rejected the only absolute banner, which was offered to you, to make all men worship you alone incontestably—the banner of earthly bread, which you rejected in the name of freedom and the bread from heaven." '

(d) *The mysterious ending to Ivan's story is given below. But before this, the Inquisitor has explained how the Church has set about* correcting *the work done by Christ by in fact basing it on 'miracle, mystery and authority' as He Himself had refused to do. He repeats his warning that on the next day the people will help to burn Him for coming to meddle with His church*

'How does your poem end?' he asked suddenly, his eyes fixed on on the ground. 'Or was that the end?'

'I intended to end it as follows: when the Inquisitor finished speaking, he waited for some time for the Prisoner's reply. His silence distressed him. He saw that the Prisoner had been listening intently to him all the time, looking gently into his face and evidently not wishing to say anything in reply. The old man would have liked him to say something, however bitter and terrible. But he suddenly approached the old man and kissed him gently on his bloodless, aged lips. That was all his answer. The old man gave a start. There was an imperceptible movement at the corners of his mouth; he went to the door, opened it and said to him: "Go, and come no more—don't come at all—never, never!" And he let him out into "the dark streets and lanes of the city". The Prisoner went away.'

'And the old man?'

'The kiss glows in his heart, but the old man sticks to his idea.'

'And you together with him?' Alyosha cried sorrowfully. 'You too?'

POINTS FOR DISCUSSION

1. D. H. Lawrence said that when he first read this story he thought that Dostoevsky was just 'showing-off in blasphemy', Later on he came to the conclusion that Dostoevsky's diagnosis of human nature was 'simple and unanswerable'. No inspiration whatever would get 'weak, impotent, vicious, worthless and rebellious man' beyond his own limits, and therefore, apart from a few saints, Christ's Christianity was doomed to failure. What do you think of this interpretation of the story?

2. Lord Eccles in his book *Half-way to Faith* comments on Lawrence's view as follows: 'I saw nothing in the argument that because an ideal is beyond our power to achieve it should therefore be discarded. If Christ's Christianity were not impossible it would soon have faded from the memory of men.' Consider this view. Where else in this book is the theme of the 'impossibility' of Christianity touched upon?

3. 'But you did not know that as soon as man rejected miracle he would at once reject God as well, for what man seeks is not so much God as miracles.' Discuss this remark of the Inquisitor.

4. 'Do you know that ages will pass and mankind will proclaim in its wisdom and science that there is no crime and therefore no sin, but that there are only hungry people?' To what extent do you think that this prophecy has come true?

5. Suggest possible interpretations of the mysterious ending of the story, when the Prisoner kisses the Inquisitor.

18. ROSE MACAULAY

THE TOWERS OF TREBIZOND

ROSE MACAULAY, who was born in 1881, was the daughter of a Cambridge lecturer and a descendant of the great Lord Macaulay. She spent many years of her childhood in Italy but later on her family returned to England and she went to Somerville College, Oxford, and read history. She wrote many novels and some travel and history books.

The Towers of Trebizond was published in 1950. Its theme is largely autobiographical, although this was not widely known at first; it tells of the conflict experienced by the leading character, Laurie, between the pull of the Anglican church and her love for a married man, whom she feels unable to give up. Rose Macaulay had herself fallen in love with a married man in 1917 when she was working in the War Office. She had been a practising Christian for several years but after struggling to maintain her religion at the same time as her friendship, she eventually broke away from the life of the church. The affair continued for almost thirty years. Towards the end of her life, however, she returned to her original faith, assisted by her friend the Reverend John Cowper Johnson, with whom she kept up a lively correspondence in the last years of her life. These letters were published after her death under the title *Last Letters to a Friend*. In one of these letters she wrote '... Trebizond stands for not merely the actual city ... but for the ideal and romantic and nostalgic vision of the Church which haunts the person who narrates the story.' Rose Macaulay died in 1958.

In the novel, Laurie, deeply involved in her conflict, has accompanied her Aunt Dot on a journey to Turkey. Aunt Dot intends to convert Turkish women to Christianity, and, as her name might imply, is a pleasantly eccentric lady; she is accompanied by a friend, Father Chantry-Pigg, a high Anglican priest. An ill-tempered camel and a semi-educated ape both figure in other parts of the story. From these background details it will already be evident that the story, for all its underlying poignancy, is told with humour and lively fantasy. Rose Macaulay wrote to Father Johnson 'Don't think my jokes, comments, speculations on religion etc. flippant will you? ... It is fundamentally a serious book, particularly the religious side of it.' In another letter she explains 'I adopted for Laurie a rather goofy, rambling prose style to put the story at one remove from myself.'

The following extracts are those parts of the book in which Laurie most clearly reveals her longings for a resolution to her dilemma. The last extract is in fact the complete final chapter of the book.

(a) *Laurie's conversation with Father Chantry-Pigg as they approach Trebizond*

Later in the morning, when I was on deck looking through glasses for the first sight of Trebizond, he came and stood by me and said, 'How much longer are you going on like this, shutting the door against God?'

This question always disturbed me; I sometimes asked it of myself, but I did not know the answer. Perhaps it would have to be for always, because I was so deeply committed to something else that I could not break away.

'I don't know,' I said.

'It's your business to know. There is no question. You must decide at once. Do you mean to drag on for years more in deliberate sin, refusing grace, denying the Holy Spirit? And when it ends, what then? It will end; such things always end. What then? Shall you come back, when it is taken out of your hands and it will cost you nothing? When you will have nothing to offer to God but a burnt out fire and a fag end? Oh, he'll take it, he'll take anything we offer. It is you who will be impoverished for ever by so poor a gift. Offer now what will cost you a great deal, and you'll be enriched beyond anything you can imagine. How do you know how much of life you still have? It may be many years, it may be a few weeks. You may leave this world without grace, go on into the next stage in the chains you won't break now. Do you ever think of that, or have you put yourself beyond caring?'

Not quite, never quite. I had tried, but never quite. From time to time I knew what I had lost. But nearly all the time, God was a bad second, enough to hurt but not to cure, to hide from but not to seek, and I knew that when I died I should hear him saying, 'Go away, I never knew you,' and that would be the end of it all, the end of everything and after that I never should know him, though then to know him would be what I should want more than anything, and not to know him would be hell. I sometimes felt this even now, but not often enough to do what would break my life to bits. Now I was vexed that Father Chantry-Pigg had brought it up and flung me into this turmoil. Hearing Mass was bad enough, hearing it and not taking part in it, seeing it and not approaching it, being offered it and shutting the door on it, and in England I seldom went.

I couldn't answer Father Chantry-Pigg, there was nothing I could say except 'I don't know'. He looked at me sternly, and said, 'I hope, I pray, that you will know before it is too late. The door won't be open for ever. Refuse it long enough, and you will become incapable of going through it. You will, little by little, stop believing. Even God can't force the soul grown blind and deaf and paralysed to see and hear and move. I beg you, in this Whitsuntide, to obey the Holy Spirit of God. That is all I have to say.'

He left me, and I stayed there at the rail, looking at the bitter Black Sea and its steep forested shores by which the Argonauts had sailed and where presently Trebizond would be seen, that corner of a lost empire, defeated and gone under so long ago that now she scarcely knew or remembered lost Byzantium, having grown unworthy of it, blind and deaf and not caring any more, not even believing, and perhaps that was the ultimate hell. Presently I should come to it; already I was on the way. It would be a refuge, that agnosticism into which I was slipping down.

POINTS FOR DISCUSSION

1. 'Offer now what will cost you a great deal, and you'll be enriched beyond anything you can imagine.' On what parts of the Gospel message does Father Chantry-Pigg seem to be basing his appeal to Laurie?

2. Father Chantry-Pigg obviously feels a sense of urgency in making his appeal. As far as you can judge from your knowledge of the human spirit, do his remarks have the ring of truth about them? Or is he applying unfair pressure to a soul in distress?

(b) *Laurie visits the ancient church of Hagia Sophia in Trebizond*

Hagia Sophia stands alone above the sea, derelict and deserted, with a tall bell tower standing near it, and I found it usually shut, except at the times when they were doing something inside it with the ladders and buckets and planks. I did not mind, because it was the outside, and particularly the south front, that I liked to look at and to paint. I would try and make out the figures on the frieze, and could do this most easily when sitting on the camel, and there were various Genesis creatures, such as Adam and Eve and the serpent, very toughly carved among trees and fruit and animals. It took me some time to make out the Greek inscription, which was about saving me from my sins, and I hesitated to say this prayer, as I did not really want to be saved from my sins, not for the time being, it would make things too difficult and too sad. I was getting into a stage when I was not quite sure what sin was, I was in a kind of fog, drifting about without clues, and this is liable to happen when you go on and on doing something, it makes a confused sort of twilight in which everything is blurred, and the next thing you know you might be stealing or anything, because right and wrong have become things you do not look at, you are afraid to, and it seems better to live in a blur. Then come the times when you wake suddenly up, and the fog breaks, and right and wrong loom through it, sharp and clear like peaks of rock, and you are on the wrong peak and know that, unless you can manage to leave it now, you may be marooned there for life and ever after. Then, as you don't leave it, the mist swirls round again, and hides the other peak, and you turn your back on it and try to forget it and succeed.

Another thing you learn about sin, it is not one deed more than another, though the Church may call some of them mortal and others not, but even the worst ones are only the result of one choice after another and part of a chain, not things by themselves, and adultery, say, is chained with stealing sweets when you are a child, or taking another child's toys, or the largest piece of cake, or letting someone else be thought to have broken something you have broken yourself, or breaking promises and telling secrets, it is all one thing and you are tied up with that chain till you break it, and the Church calls it not being in a state of grace, which means that you can get no help, so it is a vicious circle, and the odds are that you never get free. And, while I am on sin, I have often thought that it is a most strange thing that this important part of human life, the struggle that almost every one has about good and evil, cannot now be talked of without embarrassment, unless of course one is in church. It goes on just the same as it always has, for as T. S. Eliot points out,

> The world turns and the world changes,
> But one thing does not change.
> In all of my years, one thing does not change.
> However you disguise it, this thing does not change,
> The perpetual struggle of good and evil.

But now you cannot talk about it when it is your own struggle, you cannot say to your friends that you would like to be good, they would think you were going Buchmanite, or Grahamite, or something else that you would not at all care to be thought. Once people used to talk about being good and being bad, they wrote about it in letters to their friends, and conversed about it freely; the Greeks did this, and the Romans, and then, after life took a Christian turn, people did it more than ever, and all through the Middle Ages they did it, and through the Renaissance, and drama was full of it, and heaven and hell seemed for ever round the corner, with people struggling on the borderlines and never knowing which way it was going to turn out, and in which of these two states they would be spending their immortality, and this led to a lot of conversation about it all, and it was extremely interesting and exciting. And they went on talking about their conflicts all through the seventeenth and eighteenth and nineteenth centuries ... I am not sure when all this died out, but it has now become very dead. I do not remember that when I was at Cambridge we talked much about such things, they were thought rather CICCU,[1] and shunned, though we talked about everything else, such as religion, love, people, psycho-analysis, books, art, places, cooking, cars, food, sex, and all that. And still we talk about all these other things, but not about being good or bad. You can say you would like to be a good writer, or painter, or architect, or swimmer, or carpenter, or cook, or actor, or climber, or talker, or even, I suppose, a good husband or wife, but not that you would

---

[1] Cambridge Inter-Collegiate Christian Union.

like to be a good person, which is a desire you can only mention to a clergyman, whose shop it is, and who must not object or make dry answers like an unbribed oracle, but must listen and try to assist you in your vain ambition.

POINTS FOR DISCUSSION

1. Pick out the two main points Laurie makes on the subject of sin.
2. Laurie says that we cannot talk without embarrassment about 'the struggle that almost everyone has about good and evil'. Do you agree with her? If so, what do you think is implied by this embarrassment? (We do, after all, regard ourselves as being more frank and outspoken than previous generations.)

(c) *Laurie visits the Holy Land with her friend David*

... Bethlehem was charming and moving and strange, and one does not mind either there or in Jerusalem whether the shrines are rightly identified or not, because the faith of millions of pilgrims down the centuries has given them a mystical kind of reality, and one does not much mind their having been vulgarized, for this had to happen, people being vulgar and liking gaudy uneducated things round them when they pray; and one does not mind the original sites and buildings having been destroyed long ago and others built on their ruins and destroyed in their turn, again and again and again, for this shows the tenacious hold they have had on men's imaginations; they were dead but they would not lie down. Many people are troubled by the quarrels and the wars and the rivalries that raged for centuries round the Holy Sepulchre, between different sets of Christians; my mother, for instance, thought all this was a dreadful pity and disgrace, and that the whole history of the Christian Church was pretty shocking, and she liked to think that this was partly why she had left the Vicarage and my father, but really it was not this at all, but that she had grown bored and met someone else and preferred to rove about the world with him. Of course from one point of view she was right about the Church, which grew so far, almost at once, from anything which can have been intended, and became so blood-stained and persecuting and cruel and warlike and made small and trivial things so important, and tried to exclude everything not done in a certain way and by certain people, and stamped out heresies with such cruelty and rage. And this failure of the Christian Church, of every branch of it in every country, is one of the saddest things that has happened in all the world. But it is what happens when a magnificent idea has to be worked out by human beings who do not understand much of it but interpret it in their own way and think they are guided by God, whom they have not yet grasped. And yet they had grasped something, so that the Church has always had great magnificence and much courage, and people have died for it in agony, which is supposed to balance all the other people who have had to die in agony because they did not accept it, and it has flowered up in learning and culture and beauty and art, to set against its darkness and incivility and obscurantism and barbarity and nonsense, and it has produced saints and martyrs and kindness and goodness, though these have also occurred freely outside it, and it is a wonderful and most extraordinary pageant of contradictions, and I, at least, want to be inside it, though it is foolishness to most of my friends.

But what one feels in Jerusalem, where it all began, is the awful sadness and frustration and tragedy, and the great hope and triumph that sprang from it and still spring, in spite of everything we can do to spoil them with our cruelty and mean stupidity, and all the dark unchristened deeds of christened men. Jerusalem is a cruel, haunted city, like all ancient cities; it stands out because it crucified Christ; and because it was Christ we remember it with horror, but it also crucified thousands of other people, and wherever Rome (or indeed anyone else) ruled, these ghastly deaths and torturings were enjoyed by all, that is, by all except the victims and those who loved them, and it is these, the crucifixions and the flayings and the burnings and the tearing to pieces and the floggings and the blindings and the throwing to the wild beasts, all the horrors of great pain that people thought out and enjoyed, which makes history a dark pit full of serpents and terror, and out of this pit we were all dug, our roots are deep in it, and still it goes on, though all the time gradually less. And out of this ghastliness of cruelty and pain in Jerusalem on what we call Good Friday there sprang this Church that we have, and it inherited all that cruelty, which went on fighting against the love and goodness which it had inherited too, and they are still fight-

ing, but sometimes it seems a losing battle for the love and goodness, though they never quite go under and never can. And all
this grief and sadness and failure and defeat make Jerusalem
heartbreaking for Christians, and perhaps for Jews, who so often
have been massacred there by Christians, though it is more beautiful than one imagines before one sees it, and full of interest in
every street, and the hills stand round it brooding.

The Arabs stand round it too, refugees from Palestine and living
in camps, and they are brooding also, and the United Nations
and the Refugee committees feed and clothe them and try to
distract their minds, but still they brood and hate, like a sullen
army beleaguering a city, and are *sedentes in tenebris* because
they cannot go home.

On the evening after I had seen the Church of the Holy
Sepulchre, and was still feeling bemused by its complicated extra-
ordinariness, which is like nothing else in this world, I sat in the
cathedral cloisters, rather tired and a little drunk, and David
came and sat down by me, and he was a little drunk too, and more
than I was.

He said, 'How did the Sepulchre church strike you? I mean,
some people can't stand all that ornateness and tawdry glitter in
the chapels, and some people are shocked at the squabblings
between the different Churches over their different chapels—Latin
and Greek and Syrian and Coptic and Abyssinian and Armenian
and the rest, all fighting for position through the centuries and
despising each other like hell. Lots of Christians are shocked at
that. Were you?'

'No, I liked it. It's just church manners; I'm used to them. It's
only lately that Churches have even begun to think of being at all
eirenical. And I like the glitter, too. The Armenian chapel is the
best, with all those coloured witch balls and jewels and baubles
and silver and candles; it's like an Aladdin's cave. The Greek one
is pretty fine, too; it has the most incense and the best mosaics, and
what look like the most valuable candlestick and chalice. The
Franciscans seem rather drab.'

'So you think churches should be flashy?'

'Well, I like them flashy myself. Either flashy, or nobly built
and austere. There's no room for noble building in the Sepulchre
church, so they must glitter and shine. Like that little San Roque
church in Lisbon.'

'Of course you *believe* in the Church, don't you; I keep for-

getting that. Tell me, Laurie, do you really? Believe it, I mean?
It seems so fantastic.'

'It is fantastic. Why not? I like fantastic things. Believe it?
What does believe mean? You don't know, I don't know. So I
believe what I want. Anyhow, it's in the blood; I probably can't
help it.'

'As to that, it's in all our bloods. But we don't all believe it.
It's very odd, you'll admit. A Church that started up out of a
Jewish sect in Palestine nearly two thousand years ago, spread
by Jewish missionaries, catching on in the east and west, ex-
panding into this extraordinary business with a hierarchy and
elaborate doctrines and worship, growing into something entirely
unlike what its founders can have dreamed of at first, claiming
to be in communion with God, who was this young Jew in
Palestine. . . . Well, I ask you.'

I said, 'It's no good your asking me anything. I haven't got the
answers. Go and ask the Bishop. Actually, I'm pretty sleepy. But
you've left out most of it. You should read some of the liturgies
and missals. Especially the Greek. Sophia, divine wisdom, *O
Sapientia, fortiter sauviterque disponens omnia, veni ad docendum
nos.* And light. *O Oriens splendor lucis aeternae et sol justitiae,
veni el illumina sedentes in tenebris et umbra mortis.* The light
of the spirit, the light that has lighted every man who came into
the world. What I mean is, it wasn't *only* what happened in Palestine two thousand years ago, it wasn't just local and temporal and
personal, it's the other kingdom, it's the courts of God, get into
them however you can and stay in them if you can, only one can't.
But don't worry me about the Jewish Church in Palestine, or the
doings of the Christian Church ever since; it's mostly irrelevant to
what matters.'

David remembered then that he was appeasing me. He said,
'Don't mind me. You believers may be right, for all I know. All I
say, is, it's damned odd. You can't deny that it's pretty damned
odd.'

I agreed that it was pretty damned odd, and I had never tried
to say it wasn't.

'Well,' said David, still appeasing me. 'I'll get us some drinks,'
and he went inside to get these, and I sat on in the cloister, hearing
the cicadas chirp hoarsely in the garden and seeing the moon rise
up among enormous stars, and agreeing that the Church was
pretty damned odd, and I had really had quite enough drinks, for

presently I dropped to sleep, and all those gaudy jewelled chapels shimmered through my dreams, and the cicadas sawing away in the warm scented garden became hoarse chanting among drifts of incense, and nothing seemed odd any more.

Then, between sleeping and waking, there rose before me a vision of Trebizond: not Trebizond as I had seen it, but the Trebizond of the world's dreams, of my own dreams, shining towers and domes shimmering on a far horizon, yet close at hand, luminously enspelled in the most fantastic unreality, yet the only reality, a walled and gated city, magic and mystical, standing beyond my reach yet I had to be inside, an alien wanderer yet at home, held in the magical enchantment; and at its heart, at the secret heart of the city and the legend and the glory in which I was caught and held, there was some pattern that I could not unravel, some hard core that I could not make my own, and, seeing the pattern and the hard core enshrined within the walls, I turned back from the city and stood outside it, expelled in mortal grief.

POINTS FOR DISCUSSION

1. Explain what Laurie means by 'this failure of the Christian Church'. Why is she nevertheless attracted by the Church?

2. Later on Aunt Dot criticizes Laurie for her views on the Church. 'You dramatized it and yourself, you felt carried along in something aesthetically exciting and beautiful and romantic. . . .' Do you think that Laurie's view of the Church as 'a wonderful and most extraordinary pageant of contradictions' is unduly romantic? Or is it, rather, a realistic view?

3. What do you think Laurie is driving at in her remarks about 'the light that lighted every man who came into the world'? ('What I mean is, it wasn't only what happened in Palestine two thousand years ago . . . it's mostly irrelevant to what matters.')

(d) Some time after the journey to Trebizond is over, Laurie and her lover Vere are returning from a holiday together in Venice. This is the final chapter in the book

We drove from Folkestone in time to join in the great Sunday evening crawl into London. It was so different in France and Italy that after a time we began getting cross. We had meant to be up in time to dine quietly before we parted, and we felt that this would ease the parting a little. But it began to seem that we should not reach London in time for this, or for anything else. Every one had had the idea of starting for home early, so as to miss the crawl, but, since every one had had the idea, no one missed the crawl. People got peevish, they began hooting and cutting in, and I got peevish too, so I took a euphoria pill, which makes you feel as if you would get there in the end. After we were in London the buses all seemed to be rushing on against the lights for about ten seconds after they had gone red. This trick of buses, and of a lot of other drivers, but buses are the worst and the most alarming, has always made me full of rage, it is the height of meanness, stealing their turn from those with the right to cross, it is like pedestrians crossing against the lights and stealing the turn of cars which have been waiting for their chance, but this in England is not actually a legal crime, only caddish, whereas for traffic it is a legal crime as well. The taxi drivers say that when they do it they are run in if seen by the police, but that the buses usually get off, as if a driver is prosecuted the other drivers come out on strike, but this may be only the anti-police malice of taxi drivers.

When Vere was driving, I kept saying, 'Push off the moment they go green. Don't let those cads get away with it,' but Vere said, 'Better let them get away with it and stay alive.' When I took over, I was feeling like an avenging policeman, furious for the cause of legality, buoyed up by my euphorian pill, and all set to show the cads they couldn't get away with it. But they kept at it, and usually I could do nothing about it but hoot, as I was not the front car. Presently I was, and as the lights changed I saw a bus dashing up to crash the red, and I was full of rage and shouted, 'Look at the *lights*,' and started off the moment they were green. I heard Vere say, 'Famous last words,' and that was the last thing

I ever heard Vere say. The crash as the bus charged the car and hit it broadside on and smashed us was all I knew for quite a time. When I came to, everything was a mess and a crowd, and I was lying in the mess with someone sponging blood from my face. I tried to turn my head and look for Vere, and saw a figure lying in blankets close by, quite still, and the head was at an odd angle. I think I was only partly conscious, because all I said was, 'that murdering bus crashed the lights', and went off again.

They kept me in hospital a fortnight, with sprains and cuts and concussion and shock, then aunt Dot drove me down to Troutlands. The bus driver was tried for manslaughter, as so many witnesses had seen him pass the lights, but he was acquitted on the grounds of this being such common form, and only got six months for dangerous driving. He had, after all, driven no more dangerously than buses and many other vehicles drive every day, only this time he had killed someone. I do not think he was even disqualified. No one blamed me, except myself. Only I knew about that surge of rage that had sent me off, the second the lights were with me, to stop the path of that rushing monster, whose driver had thought that no one would dare to oppose him. The rage, the euphoria, the famous last words; only I knew that I and that driver had murdered Vere between us, he in selfish unscrupulousness, I in reckless anger.

I had plenty of time to think about it; no doubt my whole life. It seemed impossible to think about anything else. I don't think I talked much to aunt Dot, who nursed me back to health with the most exquisite kindness and patience. But I do not think she had ever loved any one as I had loved Vere, and nor had she killed her lover.

There were other aspects. I had come between Vere and his wife for ten years; he had given me his love, mental and physical, and I had taken it; to that extent, I was a thief. His wife knew it, but we had never spoken of it; indeed, I barely knew her. We had none of us wanted divorce, because of the children; I liked it better as it was, love and no ties. I suppose I had ruined the wife's life, because she had adored him. Vere always said that he was fonder of her because of me; men are given to saying this. But really she bored him; if she had not bored him, he would not have fallen in love with me. If I had refused to be his lover he would no doubt, sooner or later, have found someone else. But I did not refuse, or only for a short time at the beginning, and so we had ten years of it, and each year was better than the one before, love and joy gradually drowning remorse, till in the end it scarcely struggled for life. And now the joy was killed, and there seemed no reason why my life too should not run down and stop, now that its mainspring was broken. When a companionship like ours suddenly ends, it is to lose a limb, or the faculty of sight, one is, quite simply, cut off from life and scattered adrift, lacking the coherence and the integration of love. Life, I supposed, would proceed; I should see my friends, go abroad, go on with my work, such as it was, but the sentiment, enjoying principle which had kept it all ticking, had been destroyed.

I could not, all the time, believe what had happened. I would forget; and then I would remember, and say to myself, 'Vere is killed. We shan't see one another again, ever,' and it would seem a thing too monstrous to be true. John Davies of Hereford's dirge for his friend Mr. Thomas Morley kept beating in my ears like waves on a beach—

> *Death has deprived me of my dearest friend.*
> *My dearest friend is dead and laid in grave.*
> *In grave he rests until the world shall end,*
> *The world shall end, as end all things must have;*
> *All things must have an end that Nature wrought . . .*
> *Death has deprived me of my dearest friend . . .*

And so on, *ad infinitum.* In fact, I became sunk in morbid misery. If the object of pleasure be totally lost, a passion arises in the mind which is called grief. Burke: and he did not overstate.

Aunt Dot, I know, hoped that I should make my peace with the Church, now that the way was open. She spoke of it once, but with a warning note.

'I think, my dear,' she said, 'the Church used once to be an opiate to you, like that Trebizond enchanter's potion; a kind of euphoric drug. You dramatized it and yourself, you felt carried along in something aesthetically exciting and beautiful and romantic; you were a dilettante, escapist Anglican. I know you read Clement of Alexandria: do you remember where he says, "We may not be taken up and transported to our journey's end, but must travel thither on foot, traversing the whole distance of the narrow way." One mustn't lose sight of the hard core, which is, do this, do that, love your friends and like your neighbours, be just, be extravagantly generous, be honest, be tolerant, have courage, have compassion, use your wits and your imagination, understand the world you live in and be on terms with it, don't dramatize and dream and escape. Anyhow, that seems to me to be the pattern, so far as we can make it out here. So come in again with your eyes open, when you feel you can.'

But I did not feel that I could. Even the desire for it was killed. I was debarred from it less by guilt, and by what seemed to me the cheap meanness of creeping back now that the way was clear, than by revulsion from something which would divide me further from Vere. It had always tried to divide us; at the beginning, it had nearly succeeded. To turn to it now would be a gesture against the past that we had shared, and in whose bonds I was still held. 'Your church obsession,' Vere had called it. 'Well, some people have it. So long as you don't let it interfere with our lives . . .'

I had not let it do that, and now I did not want to, for a stronger obsession had won. I could not argue against the gentle mockery of that mutilated figure whom I had loved and killed. I had to be on the same side as Vere, now and for always, and in any future there might be for us.

Not that I believed now, as once I had, in any such future. Father Hugh had once said to me on the Black Sea that if one went on refusing to hear and obey one's conscience for long enough, it became stultified, and died; one stopped believing in right and wrong and in God, and all that side of life became blurred in fog: one would not even want it any more. I had got to that stage now; I wanted nothing of it, for even to think of it hurt.

Someone once said that hell would be, and now is, living without God and with evil, and being unable to get used to it. Having to do without God, without love, in utter loneliness and fear, knowing that God is leaving us alone for ever; we have driven ourselves out, we have lost God and gained hell. I live now in two hells, for I have lost God and live also without love, or without the love I want, and I cannot get used to that either. Though people say that in the end one does. To the other, perhaps never.

However this may be, I have now to make myself a life in which neither has a place. I shall go about, do my work, seek amusements, meet my friends, life will amble on, and no doubt in time I shall find it agreeable again. One is, after all, very adaptable; one has to be. One finds diversions; these, indeed, confront one at

every turn, the world being so full of natural beauties and enchant-
ing artifacts, of adventures and jokes and excitements and romance
and remedies for grief. It is simply that a dimension has been
taken out of my life, leaving it flat, not rich and rounded and
alive any more, but hollow and thin and unreal, like a ghost that
roves whispering about its old haunts, looking always for something that is not there.

The passing years will, no doubt, pacify this ghost in time. And,
when the years have all passed, there will gape the uncomfortable
and unpredictable dark void of death, and into this I shall at last
fall headlong, down and down and down, and the prospect of that
fall, that uprooting, that rending apart of body and spirit, that
taking off into so blank an unknown, drowns me in mortal fear
and mortal grief. After all, life, for all its agonies of despair and
loss and guilt, is exciting and beautiful, amusing and artful and
endearing, full of liking and of love, at times a poem and a high
adventure, at times noble and at times very gay; and whatever
(if anything) is to come after it, we shall not have this life again.

Still the towers of Trebizond, the fabled city, shimmer on a
far horizon, gated and walled and held in a luminous enchantment. It seems that for me, and however much I must stand outside them, this must for ever be. But at the city's heart lie the
pattern and the hard core, and these I can never make my own:
they are too far outside my range. The pattern should perhaps be
easier, the core less hard.

This, indeed, seems the eternal dilemma.

POINTS FOR DISCUSSION

1. Consider Aunt Dot's down-to-earth account of what the 'hard-
core' is. Bearing in mind what you know of the circumstances and
character of Laurie, do you think it was good advice?

2. What is the meaning of the quotation from Clement of Alexandria?

3. What do you think of Laurie's reaction to her grief? Do you find
anything admirable in it? Or do you think it is morbid?

4. 'The pattern should, perhaps, be easier, the core less hard.' What
does Laurie mean by this? Where else in this volume is this idea
developed more fully?

19. E. M. FORSTER

A PASSAGE TO INDIA

E. M. FORSTER was born in 1879 and was educated at Tonbridge School and at King's College, Cambridge, to which he returned later as an honorary fellow. His world-wide reputation as a major English writer rests mainly upon his five novels, of which *A Passage to India*, from which these extracts are taken, is generally recognized to be his greatest achievement. Forster made a short visit to India in 1912 and returned in 1921 to spend six months as private secretary to the Maharajah of Dewas Senior. *A Passage to India* arose out of his experiences at this time but was not published until 1924.

The novel is set in the town of Chandrapore in India, during the time of British rule. Mrs. Moore has come out from England to visit her son, Ronnie Heaslop, the district magistrate; at his request she has brought with her a young woman, Miss Adela Quested, whom Ronnie is thinking of marrying. Miss Quested is earnestly determined at all costs to see 'the real India' and not to sink into the dreary social life of the British residents, who as a result regard her as rather a crank and 'not quite pukka'. At a tea-party given by Mr. Fielding, the Principal of the local Government College and the only enlightened member of the resident white community, Miss Quested meets Aziz, a warm-hearted, volatile young Indian doctor. Dr. Aziz arranges an elaborate expedition for her and Mrs. Moore to the nearby Marabar Caves. While Miss Quested is in one of the caves, something happens which causes her to believe that she has been assaulted by Dr. Aziz, and she leaves the scene in distress and panic. Dr. Aziz is arrested and Miss Quested is a witness at his trial, which brings the latent intolerance between the races almost to the point of public hysteria. At the height of the trial Miss Quested experiences a sudden moment of illumination, and without warning confesses that she has made a mistake and withdraws the charge. Dr. Aziz is set free, and an outbreak of rioting ensues. The rest of the novel deals with the effects of this catastrophe on the relationships of those concerned. Miss Quested, now rejected by both British and Indians, returns home without marrying; Mrs. Moore has already sailed for home before the trial and has died at sea. The final section is an account of a Hindu festival during which Dr. Aziz is to some extent reconciled with his former English friends.

The novel is very much more than an account of racial prejudice in colonial India; indeed, neither of the extracts which follow have anything directly to do with the plot outlined above. *A Passage to India* is a novel of profound symbolism and psychological insight which explores the difficulties men face in their attempts to 'connect' i.e. to understand both each other and the universe. The reasons for failure to communicate are complex, but the main one seems to be what Forster calls an 'undeveloped heart'. Mrs. Moore, who does not suffer from this 'undeveloped heart,' is one of the key figures in the book. She is a Christian, but what makes her significant in Forster's eyes is her deep intuitive understanding of other people and her ability to accept them without reservation; the local inhabitants of Chandrapore, as well as Dr. Aziz, instinctively recognize this. Godbole, a professor at the Government College and a member of the Hindu priestly caste, shares this quality with Mrs. Moore, only to a much more profound degree. It is with these two characters that the extracts are concerned.

The first extract describes a crucial moment during the visit to the Marabar Caves when Mrs. Moore is overwhelmed by a sense of utter disillusionment—a sort of 'anti-vision', which annihilates rather than enhances all her values and ideals. The second extract comes from the final section of the novel and describes Professor Godbole's mystical experience during a festival at Mau which celebrates the birth of Krishna—a sort of Hindu equivalent to the birth of Jesus Christ. (Forster had himself attended one of these festivals in 1921.) In his exalted state, Godbole is able to 'connect' all his separate experiences of 'the good' into one mystical experience of love and completeness.

It must not be thought that Forster was advocating Hinduism as the one true religion. More probably Forster regarded no one religion as being fully able to comprehend all the muddle and mystery of human life. In an article[1] he once expressed the view that Protestantism had stressed the moral element at the expense of the mystical, the Hindu religion the mystical at the expense of the moral. Whether or not Forster was being fair to Protestantism as he knew it, there is certainly plenty of evidence today that people are looking for a dimension in religious experience which they have not been able to find in orthodox western Christianity.

The novel could be interpreted as an exploration of the difficulties in achieving an equilibrium between reason and emotion—and of the perils of not giving either its due. In the caves, Mrs. Moore is confronted with something 'older than the spirit', perhaps some primitive depth in the unconscious human mind which her religion had not taken into account, and thus she is unable to find any response to this vision of 'nothingness'. Yet this sense of 'nothingness' has been regularly experienced by mystics, both Christian and non-Christian, throughout the

---

[1] 'The Gods of India', *The New Weekly* (1914).

ages, and has not always been taken as a ground for nihilism, but often as a ground for saying, as Professor Godbole does in another part of the book, 'Yet absence implies presence, absence is not non-existence and we are therefore entitled to repeat "Come, come, come come." '

Professor Godbole's experience represents the other extreme. He is able to see completeness in all his experiences by uniting them in love. Even the wasp is included.

For all the effectiveness of his account of Godbole's vision, Forster seems to remain a detached and almost amused onlooker. Perhaps this is a lingering echo of his first reaction to the festival, as he describes it in some letters[2] which he sent home at the time:

'Well, what's it all about? It's called Gokul Ashtami—i.e. the 8 days feast in honour of Krishna who was born at Gokul near Muttra, and I cannot yet discover how much of it is traditional and how much due to H.H. What troubles me is that every detail, almost without exception, is fatuous and in bad-taste. The altar is a mess of little objects, stifled with rose leaves, the walls are hung with deplorable oleographs, the chandeliers, draperies—everything bad ... My memory is so bad and the muddle so great, that I forget the details of the Birth already, but the Maharajah announced it from his end of the carpet and then went to the altar and buried his face in the rose leaves, much moved. Next, a miniature cradle was set up in the aisle, and a piece of crimson silk, folded so that it looked like an old woman over whom a traction engine had passed, was laid in it and rocked by him, Bhau Sahib, the Dewan, the Finance Member, and other leading officials of the state. Noise, I need hardly add, never stopped—the great horn brayed, the cymbals clashed, the harmonium and drums did their best, while in the outer courtyard the three elephants were set to bellow and the band played 'Nights of Gladness' as loudly as possible....

I must get on to the final day—the most queer and also the most enjoyable day of the series. There was a sermon in the morning, but after it we began to play games before the altar in a ceremonial fashion; there were games of this sort in the Christian Middle Ages and they still survive in the Cathedral of Seville at Easter. With a long stick in his hand H.H. churned imaginary milk and threshed imaginary wheat and hit (I suppose) imaginary enemies and then each took a pair of little sticks, painted to match the turban, and whacked them together.... Real butter came next and was stuck on the forehead of a noble in a big lump and when he tried to lick it off another noble snatched it from behind.... I had little butter too. Then we went under a large black vessel, rather handsome, that was hung up in the aisle and we banged it with our painted sticks and the vessel broke and a mass of grain soaked in milk fell down on our heads. We fed each other with it. This was the last of the games and the mess was now awful and swarms of flies came....'

Both the following extracts should be read before attempting the points for discussion.

(a) *Mrs Moore's experience at the Marabar Caves*

The first cave was tolerably convenient. They skirted the puddle of water, and then climbed up over some unattractive stones, the sun crashing on their backs. Bending their heads, they disappeared one by one into the interior of the hills. The small black hole gaped where their varied forms and colours had momentarily functioned. They were sucked in like water down a drain. Bland and bald rose the precipices; bland and glutinous the sky that connected the precipices; solid and white, a Brahminy kite flapped between the rocks with a clumsiness that seemed intentional. Before man, with his itch for the seemly, had been born, the planet must have looked thus. The kite flapped away ... Before birds, perhaps ... And then the hole belched and humanity returned.

A Marabar cave had been horrid as far as Mrs Moore was concerned, for she had nearly fainted in it, and had some difficulty in preventing herself from saying so as soon as she got into the air again. It was natural enough: she had always suffered from faintness, and the cave had become too full, because all their retinue followed them. Crammed with villagers and servants, the circular chamber began to smell. She lost Aziz in the dark, didn't know who touched her, couldn't breathe, and some vile naked thing struck her face and settled on her mouth like a pad. She tried to regain the entrance tunnel, but an influx of villagers swept her back. She hit her head. For an instant she went mad, hitting and gasping like a fanatic. For not only did the crush and stench alarm her; there was also a terrifying echo.

Professor Godbole had never mentioned an echo; it never impressed him, perhaps. There are some exquisite echoes in India; there is the whisper round the dome at Bijapur; there are the long, solid sentences that voyage through the air at Mandu, and return unbroken to their creator. The echo in a Marabar cave is not like

these, it is entirely devoid of distinction. Whatever is said, the
same monotonous noise replies, and quivers up and down the walls
until it is absorbed in to the roof. 'Boum' is the sound as far as
the human alphabet can express it, or 'bou-oum', or 'ou-boum',—
utterly dull. Hope, politeness, the blowing of a nose, the squeak
of a boot, all produce 'boum'. Even the striking of a match starts a
little worm coiling, which is too small to complete a circle, but is
eternally watchful. And if several people talk at once, an over-
lapping howling noise begins, echoes generate echoes, and the cave
is stuffed with a snake composed of small snakes, which writhe
independently.

After Mrs Moore all the others poured out. She had given the
signal for the reflux. Aziz and Adela both emerged smiling, and
she did not want him to think his treat was a failure, so smiled
too. As each person emerged she looked for a villain, but none was
there, and she realized that she had been among the mildest
individuals whose only desire was to honour her, and that the
naked pad was a poor little baby, astride its mother's hip. Nothing
evil had been in the cave, but she had not enjoyed herself; no, she
had not enjoyed herself, and she decided not to visit a second one.

'Did you see the reflection of his match—rather pretty?' asked
Adela.

'I forget . . .'

'But he says this isn't a good cave, the best are on the Kawa
Dol.'

'I don't think I shall go on to there. I dislike climbing.'

'Very well, let's sit down again in the shade until breakfast's
ready.'

'Ah, but that'll disappoint him so; he has taken such trouble.
You should go on; you don't mind.'

'Perhaps I ought to,' said the girl, indifferent to what she did,
but desirous of being amiable.

The servants, etc., were scrambling back to the camp, pursued
by grave censures from Mohammed Latif. Aziz came to help the
guests over the rocks. He was at the summit of his powers, vigorous
and humble, too sure of himself to resent criticism, and he was
sincerely pleased when he heard they were altering his plans.
'Certainly, Miss Quested, so you and I will go together, and leave
Mrs Moore here, and we will not be long, yet we will not hurry,
because we know that will be her wish.'

'Quite right. I'm sorry not to come too, but I'm a poor walker.'

'Dear Mrs Moore, what does anything matter so long as you are my guests? I am very glad you are *not* coming, which sounds strange, but you are treating me with true frankness, as a friend.'

'Yes, I am your friend,' she said, laying her hand on his sleeve, and thinking, despite her fatigue, how very charming, how very good, he was, and how deeply she desired his happiness. 'So may I make another suggestion? Don't let so many people come with you this time. I think you may find it more convenient.'

'Exactly, exactly,' he cried, and, rushing to the other extreme, forbade all except one guide to accompany Miss Quested and him to the Kawa Dol. 'Is that all right?' he inquired.

'Quite right, now enjoy yourselves, and when you come back tell me all about it.' And she sank into the deck-chair.

If they reached the big pocket of caves, they would be away nearly an hour. She took out her writing-pad and began, 'Dear Stella, Dear Ralph,' then stopped, and looked at the queer valley and their feeble invasion of it. Even the elephant had become a nobody. Her eye rose from it to the entrance tunnel. No, she did not wish to repeat that experience. The more she thought over it, the more disagreeable and frightening it became. She minded it much more now than at the time. The crush and the smells she could forget, but the echo began in some indescribable way to undermine her hold on life. Coming at a moment when she chanced to be fatigued, it had managed to murmur, 'Pathos, piety, courage—they exist, but are identical, and so is filth. Everything exists, nothing has value.' If one had spoken vileness in that place, or quoted lofty poetry, the comment would have been the same— 'ou-boum'. If one had spoken with the tongues of angels and pleaded for all the unhappiness and misunderstanding in the world, past, present, and to come, for all the misery men must undergo whatever their opinion and position, and however much they dodge or bluff—it would amount to the same, the serpent would descend and return to the ceiling. Devils are of the North, and poems can be written about them, but no one could romanticize the Marabar because it robbed infinity and eternity of their vastness, the only quality that accommodates them to mankind.

She tried to go on with her letter, reminding herself that she was only an elderly woman who had got up too early in the morning and journeyed too far, that the despair creeping over her was merely her despair, her personal weakness, and that even if she got a sunstroke and went mad the rest of the world would go on. But suddenly, at the edge of her mind, Religion appeared, poor little talkative Christianity, and she knew that all its divine words from 'Let there be Light' to 'It is finished' only amounted to 'boum'. Then she was terrified over an area larger than usual; the universe, never comprehensible to her intellect, offered no repose to her soul, the mood of the last two months took definite form at last, and she realized that she didn't want to write to her children, didn't want to communicate with anyone, not even with God. She sat motionless with horror, and, when old Mohammed Latif came up to her, thought he would notice a difference. For a time she thought, 'I am going to be ill,' to comfort herself, then she surrendered to the vision. She lost all interest, even in Aziz, and the affectionate and sincere words that she had spoken to him seemed no longer hers but the air's.

(b) *Professor Godbole's vision at Mau*

Some hundreds of miles westward of the Marabar Hills, and two years later in time, Professor Narayan Godbole stands in the presence of God. God is not born yet—that will occur at midnight —but He has also been born centuries ago, nor can He ever be born, because He is the Lord of the Universe, who transcends human processes. He is, was not, is not, was. He and Professor Godbole stood at opposite ends of the same strip of carpet.

> 'Tukaram, Tukaram,
> Thou art my father and mother and everybody.
> Tukaram, Tukaram,
> Thou art my father and mother and everybody.
> Tukaram, Tukaram,
> Thou art my father and mother and everybody.
> Tukaram, Tukaram,
> Thou art my father and mother and everybody.
> Tukaram ...'

This corridor in the palace at Mau opened through other corridors into a courtyard. It was of beautiful hard white stucco, but its pillars and vaulting could scarcely be seen behind coloured

rags, iridescent balls, chandeliers of opaque pink glass, and murky
photographs framed crookedly. At the end was the small but
famous shrine of the dynastic cult, and the God to be born was
largely a silver image the size of a teaspoon. Hindus sat on either
side of the carpet where they could find room, or overflowed into
the adjoining corridors and the courtyard—Hindus, Hindus only,
mild-featured men, mostly villagers, for whom anything outside
their villages passed in a dream. They were the toiling ryot, whom
some call the real India. Mixed with them sat a few tradesmen out
of the little town, officials, courtiers, scions of the ruling house.
Schoolboys kept inefficient order. The assembly was in a tender,
happy state unknown to an English crowd, it seethed like a beneficent potion. When the villagers broke cordon for a glimpse of
the silver image, a most beautiful and radiant expression came
into their faces, a beauty in which there was nothing personal,
for it caused them all to resemble one another during the moment
of its indwelling, and only when it was withdrawn did they revert
to individual clods. And so with the music. Music there was, but
from so many sources that the sum-total was untrammelled. The
braying banging crooning melted into a single mass which trailed
round the palace before joining the thunder. Rain fell at intervals
throughout the night.

It was the turn of Professor Godbole's choir. As minister of
Education, he gained this special honour. When the previous
group of singers dispersed into the crowd, he pressed forward
from the back, already in full voice, that the chain of sacred
sounds might be uninterrupted. He was barefoot and in white,
he wore a pale blue turban; his gold pince-nez had caught in a
jasmine garland, and lay sideways down his nose. He and the six
colleagues who supported him clashed their cymbals, hit small
drums, droned upon a portable harmonium, and sang:

> 'Tukaram, Tukaram,
> Thou art my father and mother and everybody.
> Tukaram, Tukaram,
> Thou art my father and mother and everybody.
> Tukaram, Tukaram ...'

They sang not even to the God who confronted them, but to a
saint; they did not one thing which the non-Hindu would feel
dramatically correct; this approaching triumph of India was a
muddle (as we call it), a frustration of reason and form. Where

was the God Himself, in whose honour the congregation had
gathered? Indistinguishable in the jumble of His own altar,
huddled out of sight amid images of inferior descent, smothered
under rose-leaves, overhung by oleographs, outblazed by golden
tablets representing the Rajah's ancestors, and entirely obscured,
when the wind blew, by the tattered foliage of a banana. Hundreds of electric lights had been lit in His honour (worked by an
engine whose thumps destroyed the rhythm of the hymn). Yet His
face could not be seen. Hundreds of His silver dishes were piled
around Him with the minimum of effect. The inscriptions which
the poets of the State had composed were hung where they could
not be read, or had twitched their drawing-pins out of the stucco,
and one of them (composed in English to indicate His univer-
sality) consisted, by an unfortunate slip of the draughtsman, of the
words, 'God si Love.'

God si Love. Is this the final message of India?

'Tukaram, Tukaram ...'

continued the choir, reinforced by a squabble behind the purdah
curtain, where two mothers tried to push their children at the
same moment to the front. A little girl's leg shot out like an eel.
In the courtyard, drenched by the rain, the small Europeanized
band stumbled off into a waltz. 'Nights of Gladness' they were
playing. The singers were not perturbed by this rival, they lived
beyond competition. It was long before the tiny fragments of
Professor Godbole that attended to outside things decided that
his pince-nez was in trouble, and that until it was adjusted he
could not choose a new hymn. He laid down one cymbal, with
the other he clashed the air, with his free hand he fumbled at the
flowers round his neck. A colleague assisted him. Singing into one
another's grey moustaches, they disentangled the chain from the
tinsel into which it had sunk. Godbole consulted the music-book,
said a word to the drummer, who broke rhythm, made a thick
little blur of sound, and produced a new rhythm. This was more
exciting, the inner images it evoked more definite, and the singers'
expressions became fatuous and languid. They loved all men, the
whole universe, and scraps of their past, tiny splinters of detail,
emerged for a moment to melt into the universal warmth. Thus
Godbole, though she was not important to him, remembered an
old woman he had met in Chandrapore days. Chance brought her
into his mind while it was in this heated state, he did not select

her, she happened to occur among the throng of soliciting images, a tiny splinter, and he impelled her by this spiritual force to that place where completeness can be found. Completeness, not reconstruction. His senses grew thinner, he remembered a wasp seen he forgot where, perhaps on a stone. He loved the wasp equally, he impelled it likewise, he was imitating God. And the stone where the wasp clung—could he . . . no, he could not, he had been wrong to attempt the stone, logic and conscious effort had seduced, he came back to the strip of red carpet and discovered that he was dancing upon it. Up and down, a third of the way to the altar and back again, clashing his cymbals, his little legs twinkling, his companions dancing with him and each other. Noise, noise, the Europeanized band louder, incense on the altar, sweat, the blaze of lights, wind in the bananas, noise, thunder, eleven-fifty by his wrist-watch, seen as he threw up his hands and detached the tiny reverberation that was his soul. Louder shouts in the crowd. He danced on. The boys and men who were squatting in the aisles were lifted forcibly and dropped without changing their shapes into the laps of their neighbours. Down the path thus cleared advanced a litter.

It was the aged ruler of the State, brought against the advice of his physicians to witness the Birth ceremony.

No one greeted the Rajah, nor did he wish it; this was no moment for human glory. Nor could the litter be set down, lest it defiled the temple by becoming a throne. He was lifted out of it while its feet remained in air, and deposited on the carpet close to the altar, his immense beard was straightened, his legs tucked under him, a paper containing red powder was placed in his hand. There he sat, leaning against a pillar, exhausted with illness, his eyes magnified by many unshed tears.

He had not to wait long. In a land where all else was unpunctual, the hour of the Birth was chronometrically observed. Three minutes before it was due, a Brahman brought forth a model of the village of Gokul (the Bethlehem in that nebulous story) and placed it in front of the altar. The model was on a wooden tray about a yard square; it was of clay, and was gaily blue and white with streamers and paint. Here, upon a chair too small for him and with a head too large, sat King Kansa, who is Herod, directing the murder of some Innocents, and in a corner, similarly proportioned, stood the father and mother of the Lord, warned to depart in a dream. The model was not holy, but more than a decoration, for it diverted men from the actual image of the God, and increased their sacred bewilderment. Some of the villagers thought the Birth had occurred, saying with truth that the Lord must have been born, or they could not see Him. But the clock struck midnight, and simultaneously the rending note of the conch broke forth, followed by the trumpeting of elephants; all who had packets of powder threw them at the altar, and in the rosy dust and incense, and clanging and shouts, Infinite Love took upon itself the form of SHRI KRISHNA, and saved the world. All sorrow was annihilated, not only for Indians, but for foreigners, birds, caves, railways, and the stars; all became joy, all laughter; there had never been disease nor doubt, misunderstanding, cruelty, fear. Some jumped in the air, others flung themselves prone and embraced the bare feet of the universal lover; the women behind the purdah slapped and shrieked; the little girl slipped out and danced by herself, her black pigtails flying. Not an orgy of the body; the tradition of that shrine forbade it. But the human spirit had tried by a desperate contortion to ravish the unknown, flinging down science and history in the struggle, yes, beauty herself. Did it succeed? Books written afterwards say 'Yes.' But how, if there is such an event, can it be remembered afterwards? How can it be expressed in anything but itself? Not only from the unbeliever are mysteries hid, but the adept himself cannot retain them. He may think, if he chooses, that he has been with God, but as soon as he thinks it, it becomes history, and falls under the rules of time.

A cobra of papier mâché now appeared on the carpet, also a wooden cradle swinging from a frame. Professor Godbole approached the latter with a red silk napkin in his arms. The napkin was God, not that it was, and the image remained in the blur of the altar. It was just a napkin, folded into a shape which indicated a baby's. The Professor dandled it and gave it to the Rajah, who, making a great effort, said, 'I name this child Shri Krishna,' and tumbled it into the cradle. Tears poured from his eyes, because he had seen the Lord's salvation. He was too weak to exhibit the silk baby to his people, his privilege in former years. His attendants lifted him up, a new path was cleared through the crowd, and he was carried away to a less sacred part of the palace. There, in a room accessible to Western science by an outer staircase, his physician, Dr Aziz, awaited him. His Hindu physician, who had accompanied him to the shrine, briefly reported his symptoms.

As the ecstasy receded, the invalid grew fretful. The pumping of the steam engine that worked the dynamo disturbed him and he asked for what reason it had been introduced into his home. They replied that they would inquire, and administered a sedative.

Down in the sacred corridor, joy had seethèd to jollity. It was their duty to play various games to amuse the newly born God, and to simulate his sports with the wanton dairymaids of Brindaban. Butter played a prominent part in these. When the cradle had been removed, the principal nobles of the State gathered together for an innocent frolic. They removed their turbans, and one put a lump of butter on his forehead, and waited for it to slide down his nose into his mouth. Before it could arrive, another stole up behind him, snatched the melting morsel, and swallowed it himself. All laughed exultantly at discovering that the divine sense of humour coincided with their own. 'God si love!' There is fun in heaven. God can play practical jokes upon Himself, draw chairs away from beneath His own posteriors, set His own turbans on fire, and steal His own petticoats when He bathes. By sacrificing good taste, this worship achieved what Christianity has shirked: the inclusion of merriment. All spirit as well as all matter must participate in salvation, and if practical jokes are banned, the circle is incomplete. Having swallowed the butter, they played another game which chanced to be graceful: the fondling of Shri Krishna under the similitude of a child. A pretty red and gold ball is thrown, and he who catches it chooses a child from the crowd, raises it in his arms, and carries it round to be caressed. All stroke the darling creature for the Creator's sake, and murmur happy words. The child is restored to his parents, the ball thrown on, and another child becomes for a moment the World's Desire. And the Lord bounds hither and thither through the aisles, chance, and the sport of chance, irradiating little mortals with His immortality. . . . When they had played this long enough —and being exempt from boredom, they played it again and again, they played it again and again—they took many sticks and hit them together, whack smack, as though they fought the Pandava wars, and threshed and churned with them, and later on they hung from the roof of the temple, in a net, a great black earthenware jar, which was painted here and there with red, and wreathed with dried figs. Now came a rousing sport. Springing up, they struck at the jar with their sticks. It cracked, broke, and a mass of greasy rice and milk poured on to their faces. They ate and smeared one another's mouths, and dived between each other's legs for what had been pashed upon the carpet. This way and that spread the divine mess, until the line of schoolboys, who had somewhat fended off the crowd, broke for their share. The corridors, the courtyard, were filled with benign confusion. Also the flies awoke and claimed their share of God's bounty. There was no quarrelling, owing to the nature of the gift, for blessed is the man who confers it on another, he imitates God. And those 'imitations', those 'substitutions', continued to flicker through the assembly for many hours, awaking in each man, according to his capacity, an emotion that he would not have had otherwise. No definite image survived; at the Birth it was questionable whether a silver doll or a mud village, or a silk napkin, or an intangible spirit, or a pious resolution had been born. Perhaps all these things! Perhaps none! Perhaps all birth is an allegory! Still, it was the main event of the religious year. It caused strange thoughts. Covered with grease and dust, Professor Godbole had once more developed the life of his spirit. He had, with increasing vividness, again seen Mrs Moore, and found her faintly clinging forms of trouble. He was a Brahman, she Christian, but it made no difference, it made no difference whether she was a trick of his memory or a telepathic appeal. It was his duty, as it was his desire, to place himself in the position of the God and to love her, and to place himself in her position and to say to the God, 'Come, come, come, come.' This was all he could do. How inadequate! But each according to his own capacities, and he knew that his own were small. 'One old Englishwoman and one little, little wasp,' he thought, as he stepped out of the temple into the grey of a pouring wet morning. 'It does not seem much, still it is more than I am myself.'

POINTS FOR DISCUSSION

1. 'Religion is simply not all sweetness and light; there are long stretches of *accidie* to be gone through, the "dark night of the soul". Call it what you will, this factor must be taken seriously in any account of religion.' What examples can you recall from the Old and New Testaments of the sort of sense of desolation which Mrs Moore

experienced at the Marabar Caves? Are there any examples in the other extracts in this book?

2. Have you ever considered that Christianity as presented today is too concerned with ethics? To what extent do you think that the Christian message is concerned with morals and conduct?

3. Compare Forster's two accounts of the Gokul Ashtami festival. What main differences do you notice? What attitudes of mind governed his first reaction?

4. Is it a fair comment that Christianity has 'shirked the inclusion of merriment'. (Do not confine your discussion to this country, or to this century.)

5. What evidence do you know of in the New Testament that Christians believe in the ultimate reconciliation of all things? Is this theme re-echoed in any of the others extracts in this book?

6. 'A characteristic defect of the self-consciously liberal and enlightened approach to life is the belief that we are all innocuous and reasonable at heart, that we actually *are* only what we care to know about ourselves. This is far too simple a view of the human psyche; there are depths in the unconscious mind which can overwhelm us, and to be unable through fear or fastidiousness to acknowledge this is to be out of touch with the facts of life.' Are we in danger of over-intellectualizing our religion? In what ways does the deeper and more instinctive part of the mind find expression in western Christianity today?